Second Edition

STRATEGIES FOR
Content Area Learning

VOCABULARY ● COMPREHENSION ● RESPONSE

Jerry L. Johns

Roberta L. Berglund

KENDALL/HUNT PUBLISHING COMPANY
4050 Westmark Drive Dubuque, Iowa 52002
www.kendallhunt.com/readingresources.html

Project Team
Chairman and Chief Executive Officer: Mark C. Falb
Senior Vice President, College Division: Thomas W. Gantz
Director of National Book Program: Paul B. Carty
Editorial Development Manager: Georgia Botsford
Vice President, Production and Manufacturing: Alfred C. Grisanti
Assistant Vice President, Production Services: Christine E. O'Brien
Prepress Project Coordinator: Carrie Maro
Cover Designer: Jenifer Chapman

Author Information for Correspondence and Workshops

Jerry L. Johns, Ph.D.
Consultant in Reading
E-mail: *jjohns@niu.edu*

Roberta L. Berglund, Ed.D.
Consultant in Reading/Language Arts
E-mail: *readboulder@yahoo.com*

Ordering Information

Address: Kendall/Hunt Publishing Company
4050 Westmark Drive, P.O. Box 1840
Dubuque, IA 52004-1840

Telephone: 800-247-3458, Ext. 4

Web site: www.kendallhunt.com

Fax: 800-772-9165

Cover image © 2006 by DigitalVision.

Printed in the United States of America

10 9 8 7 6 5 4 3

Preface and Overview

Who Will Use This Book?

We have written this practical and useful book for a wide range of professionals in middle and high schools, including content area teachers and those working with struggling learners. The book is ideal for school, district, and other types of professional development programs. It will also be a helpful supplement in undergraduate and graduate reading and language arts classes as well as in clinical courses where there is a desire to provide useful strategies that have wide applicability across the content areas. Professors teaching content area courses will find the book especially valuable.

What Are Some of the Outstanding Qualities of This Book?

There are several outstanding qualities of this book.

1. The book contains strategies that have utility across the curriculum.
2. The strategies are organized around three important areas: vocabulary, comprehension, and response.
3. The strategies are presented with a unique and helpful chart that quickly shows when, why, and how to use them. The type of text (narrative or informational) with which the strategy can be used is also indicated.
4. The strategies are presented in an easy-to-follow, step-by-step manner.
5. Most of the strategies contain one or more examples from the various content areas that comprise the curriculum.
6. A reproducible master accompanies most strategies.
7. A CD-ROM contains all the reproducibles in the book plus extra reproducibles, a bonus strategy, and websites (Appendix B).

What Grade Levels Do the Strategies Address?

The strategies in this book are relevant for the middle grades through high school. After reading about a strategy, it should be quite easy for you to determine how best to use it with your students. You will probably want to adapt some of the strategies to fit your teaching style, text materials, and your students' particular needs.

What Insights Have Been Provided by Research?

There is little doubt that teaching results in student learning. A persistent problem is that of teachers mentioning a skill or assigning a task without taking the time to teach it. Instruction that is characterized by clear explanation, modeling, and guided practice can increase student learning. The National Reading Panel (2000) compiled a large volume that offers several strategies for effective comprehension instruction. According to Cunningham (2001), the comprehension section of the report is potentially valuable. The following principles are generally consistent with two other major reviews (Pearson & Fielding, 1991; Tierney & Cunningham, 1984) and a related chapter (Pressley, 2000) of research on teaching comprehension.

1. Teach students to be aware of their own comprehension. This strategy is often referred to as comprehension monitoring.
2. Have students work together on their strategies. This strategy is called cooperative learning.

3. Have students make graphic summaries of what is read through the use of graphic and semantic organizers.
4. Use story and text structure.
5. Help students learn to ask and answer questions.
6. Teach students to summarize what is read.

The strategies selected for this book will help you in each of these areas. The key ingredients, however, are your actions as the teacher. Consider the following model.

I do	I do	You do	You do
You watch	You help	I help	I watch

- Take time to teach the strategies.
- Tell students how the strategies will help them become better readers.
- Gradually release the responsibility to students.
- Model how the strategies are used.
- Think aloud by describing what goes on in your mind as you are using the strategy.
- Provide guided practice so students can learn how the strategy will help them understand the lesson or text.
- Reinforce their efforts.
- Develop the strategies over time and remind students to use their strategies in a variety of contexts.
- Have students reflect on the strategies and how they help in particular contexts.

Finally, we want to stress again the critical importance of teaching the strategies.

Is This Book Easy to Use?

Yes! The format and organization of this book makes it very user friendly. We have also included a Quick Reference Guide inside the front cover so you can quickly locate the various strategies and consider their use. Note that the strategies are listed in alphabetical order. There is also a reference page on the back cover.

Where Should I Begin?

Glance at the Quick Reference Guide inside the front cover. Scan the strategies and find a particular strategy that interests you. Turn to the page for that strategy. Suppose you select the Discussion Web on page 35. Under the title, you will see a chart that covers five areas.

FOCUS	TEXT	WHEN	WHY	HOW
Vocabulary	✓Narrative	Before Reading	Connecting Questioning	Individual
✓Comprehension	✓Informational	During Reading	✓Synthesizing ✓Inferring	✓Small Group
✓Response		✓After Reading	✓Determining Importance	✓Whole Group

1. **FOCUS** indicates how many of the three areas (i.e., vocabulary, comprehension, and response) are covered by the strategy. The two check marks indicate that the Discussion Web focuses on *comprehension* and *response*. Response indicates that oral or written actions by students are part of this strategy.

2. **TEXT** refers to the two major classifications of materials: narrative and informational. The two check marks indicate that the Discussion Web can be used with both types of text.

3. **WHEN** tells you if you should use the strategy before, during, and/or after reading. The check mark indicates that the Discussion Web is best used *after* reading.

4. **WHY** is based on five of the major areas Keene and Zimmermann (1997) discuss in *Mosaic of Thought*. The areas are based on the work of Pearson, Roehler, Dole, and Duffy (1992). These areas help students become thoughtful, independent readers who are engaged in their reading and learning. Following are brief descriptions of the five areas we use in this resource.

   - *Connecting*—Students increase their comprehension when they think about how their lives are connected to the text and to the world.
   - *Questioning*—Asking questions engages students in an internal dialogue to clarify understanding.
   - *Synthesizing*—Students use new information and their prior knowledge to create thoughts or perspectives.
   - *Inferring*—Students use what is known as well as clues from the text to contemplate and hypothesize about what was read.
   - *Determining Importance*—Students learn to identify the important ideas in printed materials and separate them from ideas that are less important.

5. **HOW** refers to whether the strategy is best used with individuals, small groups, and/or whole groups. You can see that the Discussion Web is best used with *small groups* and *whole groups*. There is amazing variety in how the strategies can be used, so don't be limited by the check marks. You'll likely find additional ways to use the strategies that increase student engagement.

Discussion Web

FOCUS	TEXT	WHEN	WHY	HOW
Vocabulary	✓Narrative	Before Reading	Connecting Questioning	Individual
✓Comprehension	✓Informational	During Reading	✓Synthesizing ✓Inferring	✓Small Group
✓Response		✓After Reading	✓Determining Importance	✓Whole Group

DESCRIPTION

The Discussion Web (Alvermann, 1991; Duthie, 1986) is a graphic aid for helping students address both sides of an issue by considering pro and con arguments before drawing a conclusion. Active discussion is stimulated by this strategy, which incorporates reading, speaking, listening, and writing.

Procedure

1. Choose a selection that has the potential to generate opposing viewpoints. Be sure to initially develop an understanding of key vocabulary, survey illustrations and charts, build background knowledge as needed, and help students set purposes for reading. Then have students read the selection.

2. Make an overhead transparency of the reproducible master on page 39 and duplicate and distribute copies to students. Use the transparency on the overhead projector to introduce the Discussion Web. Pose a question related to the selection that stimulates opposing views and have students write the question on their Discussion Web.

3. Have students work with a partner to brainstorm at least three responses for each side of the question posed. Encourage students to write down key words or phrases and strive to have an equal number of reasons in each column. Students could take turns writing reasons on the same Discussion Web. Provide ample time for each set of partners to share their reasons.

4. Pair one set of partners with another set of partners so they can compare their reasons. Tell the groups that the goal is to work toward consensus. Provide time for students to share and discuss. Encourage students to listen carefully, especially for views that may differ from their own. The conclusion can be written in the box on the bottom of the sheet.

35

Below the chart are the words *Description* and *Procedure*. There is a brief description of the Discussion Web followed by a step-by-step procedure for using it. We like to think of the numbered steps as a systematic lesson plan to help you present the strategy to your students. You should, of course, feel free to adapt the steps and examples to fit your students.

We then provide one or more *examples* (see the next page) of how the strategy might be used in different subjects or content areas. You may quickly be able to think of logical extensions to your lessons in a variety of areas.

To make the strategy especially useful, a *reproducible master* is included for most of the strategies. You have the publisher's permission to reproduce and use the master with your students within the guidelines noted on the copyright page of this book.

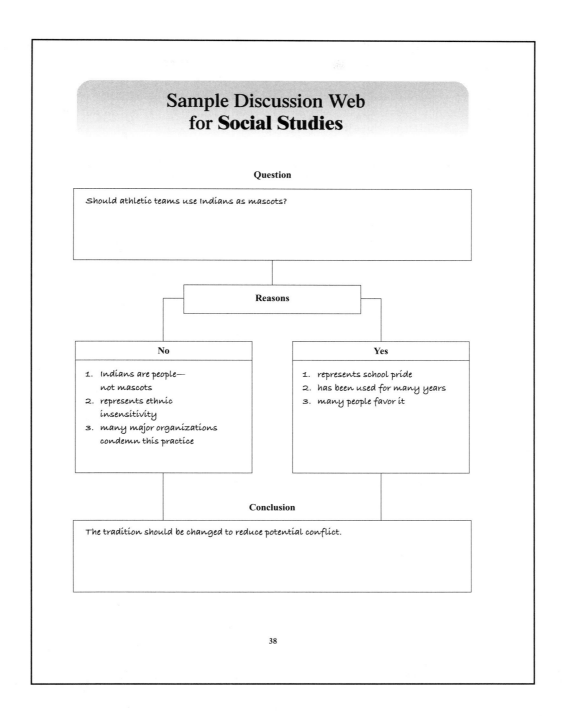

Sample Discussion Web for Social Studies

Question

Should athletic teams use Indians as mascots?

Reasons

No

1. Indians are people—not mascots
2. represents ethnic insensitivity
3. many major organizations condemn this practice

Yes

1. represents school pride
2. has been used for many years
3. many people favor it

Conclusion

The tradition should be changed to reduce potential conflict.

38

References

Cunningham, J. W. (2001). The National Reading Panel Report (Essay Book Review). *Reading Research Quarterly, 36,* 326–335.

Keene, E. O., & Zimmermann, S. (1997). *Mosaic of thought.* Portsmouth, NH: Heinemann.

National Reading Panel. (2000). *Teaching children to read: An evidence-based assessment of the scientific research literature on reading and its implications for reading instruction.* Washington, DC: National Institute for Child Health & Human Development.

Pearson, P. D., & Fielding, L. (1991). Comprehension instruction. In R. Barr, M. L. Kamil, P. B. Mosenthal, & P. D. Pearson (Eds.), *Handbook of reading research* (Vol. II) (pp. 815–816). White Plains, NY: Longman.

Pearson, P. D., Roehler, L. R., Dole, J. A., & Duffy, G. G. (1992). Developing expertise in reading comprehension. In S. J. Samuels & A. E. Farstrup (Eds.), *What research has to say about reading instruction* (pp. 153–169). Newark, DE: International Reading Association.

Pressley, M. (2000). What should comprehension instruction be the instruction of? In M. L. Kamil, P. B. Mosenthal, P. D. Pearson, & R. Barr (Eds.), *Handbook of reading research* (Vol. III) (pp. 545–561). Mahwah, NJ: Erlbaum.

Tierney, R. J., & Cunningham, J. W. (1984). Research on teaching reading comprehension. In P. D. Pearson, R. Barr, M. L. Kamil, & P. Mosenthal (Eds.), *Handbook of reading research* (Vol. I) (pp. 609–655). White Plains, NY: Longman.

About the Authors

Jerry L. Johns has been recognized as a distinguished professor, writer, and outstanding teacher educator. His career was spent at Northern Illinois University along with visiting professorships at the University of Victoria in British Columbia and Western Washington University. He has taught students from kindergarten through college. Dr. Johns now serves as a consultant and speaker to schools and professional organizations.

Dr. Johns is a past president of the International Reading Association, Illinois Reading Council, College Reading Association, and Northern Illinois Reading Council. He has received recognition for outstanding service to each of these professional organizations and is a member of the Illinois Reading Council Hall of Fame. Dr. Johns has served on numerous committees of the International Reading Association (IRA) and was a member of the Board of Directors. He has also received the Outstanding Teacher Educator in Reading Award from the International Reading Association.

Dr. Johns has been invited to consult, conduct workshops, and make presentations for teachers and professional groups throughout the United States and in seven countries. He has also prepared nearly 300 publications and more than twenty books that have been useful to a diverse group of educators. His *Basic Reading Inventory,* now in its ninth edition, is widely used in undergraduate and graduate classes, as well as by practicing teachers. Dr. Johns recently coauthored the fourth edition of *Improving Reading: Strategies and Resources,* the second edition of *Improving Writing, Visualization: Using Mental Images to Strengthen Comprehension,* and the third edition of *Fluency: Strategies & Assessments.*

Roberta L. (Bobbi) Berglund has had a long and distinguished career in education. Her public school experience spans more than 20 years and includes serving as a classroom teacher, reading specialist, Title I Director, and a district curriculum administrator. Dr. Berglund has been a member of the reading faculty at the University of Wisconsin-Whitewater and has also taught graduate reading courses at Northern Illinois University, Rockford College, National-Louis University, and Aurora University. Currently Dr. Berglund is a consultant in the area of reading and language arts, working with school districts and regional offices of education in developing curriculum and assessment, conducting staff development, and guiding the selection of instructional materials for reading, spelling, writing, and related areas.

Dr. Berglund has received honors for outstanding service to several organizations and has been selected as a member of the Illinois Reading Council Hall of Fame. She also was honored with the Those Who Excel Award from the Illinois State Board of Education. Dr. Berglund has served on several committees of the International Reading Association including the program committee for the World Congress in Scotland and as chair of the Publications Committee.

Dr. Berglund has conducted numerous workshops for teachers and has been invited to make presentations at state, national, and international conferences. She is the author of over fifty publications and is the coauthor of seven professional books, including the third edition of *Fluency: Strategies and Assessments.*

Anticipation/Reaction Guide

FOCUS	TEXT	WHEN	WHY	HOW
Vocabulary	✓Narrative	✓Before Reading	✓Connecting ✓Questioning	✓Individual
✓Comprehension	✓Informational	During Reading	✓Synthesizing ✓Inferring	Small Group
✓Response		✓After Reading	Determining Importance	✓Whole Group

DESCRIPTION

The Anticipation/Reaction Guide (Herber, 1978) is a series of statements about a selection. If the statements serve as an Anticipation Guide, students' thoughts and opinions are sought prior to reading the selection. If the statements serve as a Reaction Guide, students evaluate the statements in relationship to the selection they have read. Using the statements before and after reading would be an Anticipation/Reaction guide, and students respond to the statements prior to and after reading.

Procedure

1. Decide which variation of the Anticipation/Reaction Guide you will use. The strategy is commonly used with informational materials, but it can also be used with narrative materials.

2. Identify the major ideas or concepts in the materials and create five to seven statements related to them. Try to create statements that challenge or support students' preconceived notions related to the major ideas or concepts in the materials to be read.

3. Write the statements on one of the Anticipation/Reaction Guide reproducible masters on pages 4 or 5, duplicate it, and distribute it to students. The remaining steps in this section describe how to present an Anticipation/Reaction Guide.

4. Distribute a copy of the Anticipation/Reaction Guide to each student. For instructional purposes, you may also want to make a transparency of the guide distributed to students.

5. Direct students' attention to the statements on the guide and have them look at the Before Reading column. Tell them that they should read the statements and check those with which they agree prior to reading the selection. Ask them if the statements remind them of something they already know about.

6. After students have completed the Before Reading column, have them discuss the statements. The discussion could take place in small groups or with the whole class. Then have students read the selection upon which the statements are based.

7. After students have read the selection, they should complete the After Reading column. Stress that students should base their responses in the After Reading column on information from the selection. Ask students how the connections or questions they made prior to reading helped them to better understand the selection.

8. Engage students in a follow-up discussion to determine whether their ideas have changed and why. Encourage students to use information from the selection to support their ideas. Help students understand that it is common for their ideas to change as a result of reading and discussing the selection.

9. Seek ways to use each of the three types of guides with a variety of reading selections. Consider using variety in the words for the columns that students check. Possible words are provided below.

Before Reading	After Reading
Agree	Disagree
Tend to Agree	Tend to Disagree
True	False
Likely	Unlikely
Yes	No
Fact	Opinion

10. An alternative approach is to have students complete the Before Reading column independently. Then designate one side of the room "True" and the other side of the room "False." After each statement is read aloud, have students move about the room to indicate whether they believe the answer is true or false. Invite discussion and interaction.

Additional samples can be found on the CD-ROM accompanying this book.

Reference

Herber, H. L. (1978). *Teaching reading in content areas* (2nd ed.). Upper Saddle River, NJ: Prentice Hall.

Sample Anticipation Guide
for **Science**

❄ **DIRECTIONS**

Before you read the booklet *Summer Health Guide,* read the statements below and check those with which you agree. We will then discuss the statements in small groups

Before Reading

Agree	Disagree	
	✓	1. Experts say even one bad sunburn during childhood or teenage years can double your risk of getting skin cancer as an adult.
✓		2. Gray, green, and brown sunglass lenses are the best.
	✓	3. A wet T-shirt can protect you from getting sunburned.
✓		4. The best time to apply sunscreen is when you first go out into the sun.
	✓	5. If your sunscreen has an SPF (sun protection factor) of 10, that means you can stay out in the sun for 10 hours.
✓		6. The sun's rays can damage your vision over time.
✓		7. The more you pay for sunglasses, the better they protect your eyes.
	✓	8. Skin cancer is the fastest growing type of cancer.
	✓	9. If you are taking medication for acne, an infection, or birth control, your skin and eyes can be more sensitive to the sun's rays.
✓		10. The darker the sunglass lenses, the more protection you get from the sun's ultraviolet rays.
✓		11. Nonwhite teens don't need to use sunscreen.
✓		12. Sunglasses with polarizing lenses are best for skiing and water sports.

Name _____ Date _____

⊛ Anticipation/ReactionGuide

Selection Title _____

❏ **Anticipation Guide**
   Before Reading

❏ **Reaction Guide**
   After Reading

Agree	Disagree		Agree	Disagree
_____	_____	1. _____	_____	_____
		_____		
		_____		
_____	_____	2. _____	_____	_____
		_____		
		_____		
_____	_____	3. _____	_____	_____
		_____		
		_____		
_____	_____	4. _____	_____	_____
		_____		
		_____		
_____	_____	5. _____	_____	_____
		_____		
		_____		
_____	_____	6. _____	_____	_____
		_____		
		_____		
_____	_____	7. _____	_____	_____
		_____		
		_____		

Based on Herber (1978). From Jerry L. Johns and Roberta L. Berglund, *Strategies for Content Area Learning* (2nd ed.).
Copyright © 2006 by Kendall/Hunt Publishing Company (1-800-247-3458, ext. 4). May be reproduced for
noncommercial educational purposes. www.kendallhunt.com/readingresources.html

Name _____ Date _____

⊛ Anticipation/Reaction Guide

Selection Title _____

❏ **Anticipation Guide**
   Before Reading

❏ **Reaction Guide**
   After Reading

Agree	Disagree		Agree	Disagree
_____	_____	1. _____	_____	_____

Why do you agree or disagree? _____
_____

| _____ | _____ | 2. _____ | _____ | _____ |

Why do you agree or disagree? _____
_____

| _____ | _____ | 3. _____ | _____ | _____ |

Why do you agree or disagree? _____
_____

| _____ | _____ | 4. _____ | _____ | _____ |

Why do you agree or disagree? _____
_____

| _____ | _____ | 5. _____ | _____ | _____ |

Why do you agree or disagree? _____
_____

Based on Herber (1978). From Jerry L. Johns and Roberta L. Berglund, *Strategies for Content Area Learning* (2nd ed.).
Copyright © 2006 by Kendall/Hunt Publishing Company (1-800-247-3458, ext. 4). May be reproduced for
noncommercial educational purposes. www.kendallhunt.com/readingresources.html

Before-During-After (B-D-A)

FOCUS	TEXT	WHEN	WHY	HOW
Vocabulary	Narrative	✓Before Reading	✓Connecting ✓Questioning	✓Individual
✓Comprehension	✓Informational	✓During Reading	✓Synthesizing Inferring	✓Small Group
Response		✓After Reading	Determining Importance	✓Whole Group

DESCRIPTION

The Before-During-After (B-D-A) strategy (Laverick, 2002) is an adaptation of the well-established and popular K-W-L strategy (Ogle, 1986). B-D-A focuses on the essential components of effective reading and encourages students to use the proficient reader strategies of predicting, focusing, note taking, summarizing, and determining the main idea before, during, and after reading. Laverick developed the B-D-A strategy to provide guidance to adolescents in helping them to focus on and internalize information from text.

Procedure

1. Duplicate copies of the B-D-A reproducible on page 10 and distribute them to students.

2. Before reading, invite students to brainstorm and list what is known about the topic to be studied. This can be done individually, in student partner teams, or as a whole group. The brainstormed ideas should be listed under the "Before" column on the strategy form.

3. Explain to students that as they read the selection, they need to note new information under the "During" column. This can be done individually, with partners, or in small groups. Tell students that they need to put a plus (+) next to statements in the "Before" column if they are found to be correct.

4. When students finish reading, invite them to briefly summarize the information under the "After" column. Students can share their summaries in small groups or with the whole class.

5. When students have shared and possibly revised their summaries, have them review the information in the "Before" column. Note those items that were found to be accurate. Discuss with students how they might determine the accuracy of ideas shared that weren't confirmed or disconfirmed by the reading.

6. Instruct students to develop three questions and write them in the "After" column. These questions should be those that could be answered by students who have read the text. If students have worked with Question-Answer Relationships (see page 107), you may want to have them develop questions in each of the QAR categories. If the answers to the questions can be located in a specific place in the text, have students note the page number next to the question.

7. In small- or whole-group discussion, students should share their questions and invite their colleagues to answer them.

8. Finally, work with the whole group to develop a one-sentence main idea.

References

Laverick, C. (2002). B-D-A strategy: Reinventing the wheel can be a good thing. *Journal of Adolescent and Adult Literacy, 46,* 144–147.

Ogle, D. (1986). K-W-L: A teaching model that develops active reading of expository text. *The Reading Teacher, 39,* 564–570.

⬛★ Before-During-After (B-D-A)

Name ___Anna___ Date ___January 11___

Title ___Greece___

Before	During	After
What I Think I Know About This Topic	**What's New**	**My Summary and Three Questions**
+ - Europe	- part of Balkan Peninsula	This was about . . .
+ - center of ancient civilization	- major industries	Greece is a small European country whose history has influenced much of the Western World. It is a diverse land of urban and rural, mountains and seacoast, old world and modern cultures.
+ - Athens—capital	- tourism	
+ - windmills	- shipping	
+ - Parthenon	- oil refining	
- home of Olympic Games	- food stuffs	1. How has ancient Greece influenced us today?
- larger than Italy	- earthquake prone	2. What is the capital city? (p. 116)
	- many islands	
	- Greek Orthodox religion	3. What might a visitor to Greece expect to see?
	- Euro is currency	
	- people speak Greek	

Here's the main idea in one sentence: ___This selection provided basic information about Greece.___

⊛ Before-During-After (B-D-A)

Name _____ Date _____

Title _____

Before	During	After
What I Think I Know About This Topic	What's New	My Summary and Three Questions
		This was about . . .
		1.
		2.
		3.

Here's the main idea in one sentence: _____

_____

_____

Bookmarks

FOCUS	TEXT	WHEN	WHY	HOW
✓Vocabulary	✓Narrative	Before Reading	✓Connecting ✓Questioning	✓Individual
✓Comprehension	✓Informational	✓During Reading	✓Synthesizing Inferring	Small Group
✓Response		After Reading	✓Determining Importance	Whole Group

DESCRIPTION

Bookmarks (Beers, 2003; Daniels & Zemelman, 2004) give students a place to record brief thoughts while reading. When students record their thoughts on the Bookmarks, they become active readers who make connections, ask questions, and determine important ideas. Bookmarks can also be used for recording key concepts or vocabulary words that are significant to the reading.

Procedure

1. Make an overhead transparency and duplicate copies of the Bookmarks reproducible master on page 13, using card stock or paper. You may also have students create their own by folding a piece of paper in thirds.
2. Select an excerpt from a text that your students will be asked to read.
3. Read a portion of the text aloud and model on an overhead transparency what kinds of thoughts can be recorded on Bookmarks. Try to provide examples that include a variety of responses: personal connections, questions, important passages, and key terminology.
4. Distribute copies of the Bookmarks or have students fold a piece of paper in thirds. Then have students continue reading from the text. Have students record their thoughts on the Bookmarks as they read.
5. Invite students to discuss their responses with a partner or in collaborative groups.
6. Encourage whole group sharing to identify the variety of responses students recorded while reading.
7. Bookmarks can also be used after reading to help students recall their understanding of the selected text.

References

Beers, K. (2003). *When kids can't read: What teachers can do.* Portsmouth, NH: Heinemann.

Daniels, H., & Zemelman, S. (2004). *Subjects matter: Every teacher's guide to content-area reading.* Portsmouth, NH: Heinemann.

Sample Bookmarks for
Middle School Social Studies

Name: Amy

Topic: Louisiana Purchase

—Robert Livingston and James Monroe negotiated the purchase.

—What would have happened if Napoleon decided not to sell the Louisiana Territory?

—I think at the time, $15 million was a lot of money for the purchase. The aftermath of Hurricane Katrina will cost much more.

—How much land did the U.S. actually acquire?

—I now understand how the "French Quarter" in New Orleans got its name.

—How much money did the federal government give Lewis and Clark for their expedition?

Name: Amy

Topic: Louisiana Purchase

Vocabulary Word: cede

Page 362

to grant or give up land

Vocabulary Word: Louisiana Territory

Page 362

Land from the Mississippi River west to the Rocky Mountains

Vocabulary Word: constructionists

Page 363

those who believed that the federal government can only do what the Constitution says, nothing more

Vocabulary Word: envoy

Page 363

a diplomat sent to negotiate the purchase

Vocabulary Word: _____

Page _____

# Bookmarks

Name: _____	Name: _____
Topic: _____	Topic: _____
	Vocabulary Word: _____
	Page ____
	Vocabulary Word: _____
	Page ____
	Vocabulary Word: _____
	Page ____
	Vocabulary Word: _____
	Page ____
	Vocabulary Word: _____
	Page ____

Character Feelings and Traits

FOCUS	TEXT	WHEN	WHY	HOW
Vocabulary	✓Narrative	Before Reading	Connecting Questioning	✓Individual
✓Comprehension	✓Informational	During Reading	✓Synthesizing ✓Inferring	✓Small Group
✓Response		✓After Reading	Determining Importance	✓Whole Group

DESCRIPTION

Character Feelings and Traits (Johns & Lenski, 2005) can be used with fictional characters and historical or living individuals. Students are asked to identify feelings or traits (or both) of fictional and real individuals and offer support for the feelings and traits identified through an analysis of printed materials (e.g., a story, a section of text, a newspaper article, or historical documents).

Procedure

1. Write the words *feelings* and *traits* on the board or on an overhead transparency. Help students understand that *feelings* are emotions, sentiments, or desires and that *traits* are distinguishing features of the character or individual.

2. Have students get in small groups to identify specific feelings and traits. After about three minutes, have students share their words and write them under the proper category. A partial example is shown below.

Feelings	**Traits**
happy	honest
pleased	hard working
anxious	dishonest
nervous	creative

3. Help students understand that some words may characterize both feelings and traits. For example, nervous is usually a feeling, but it could also be a trait that characterizes a particular individual.

4. Identify a particular reading selection (narrative or informational) for which the Character Feelings and Traits reproducible masters (pages 18–19) would be appropriate. Decide if you will use feelings, traits, or both.

5. After reading, have students write the name of the individual in the oval. Then have students review the selection and decide upon some feelings and/or traits. These words can be written on the arrowed line. Students should then support the words they chose with information from the selection.

6. Provide time for students to discuss their responses in small groups. If there are several characters in a story or play, students might select one of the characters and complete the sheet. Small groups of students could then share their thoughts about the same characters. If a current or historical individual is the focus of the selection, a whole group discussion could be used.

Reference

Johns, J. L., & Lenski, S. D. (2005). *Improving reading: Strategies and resources* (4th ed.). Dubuque, IA: Kendall/Hunt.

Sample Character Feelings
for Middle School **Language Arts**

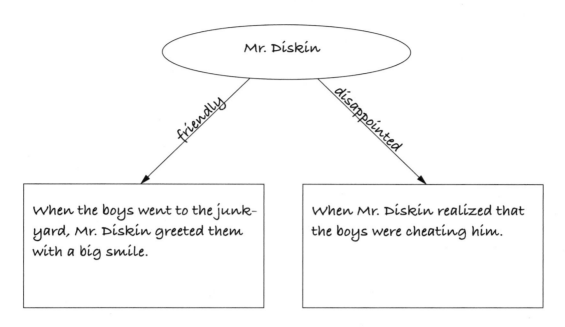

Mr. Diskin

friendly

disappointed

When the boys went to the junk-yard, Mr. Diskin greeted them with a big smile.

When Mr. Diskin realized that the boys were cheating him.

Sample Character Traits
for **Social Studies**

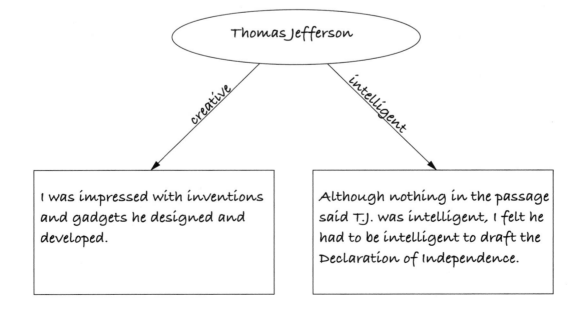

Thomas Jefferson

creative

intelligent

I was impressed with inventions and gadgets he designed and developed.

Although nothing in the passage said T.J. was intelligent, I felt he had to be intelligent to draft the Declaration of Independence.

Name _____ Date _____

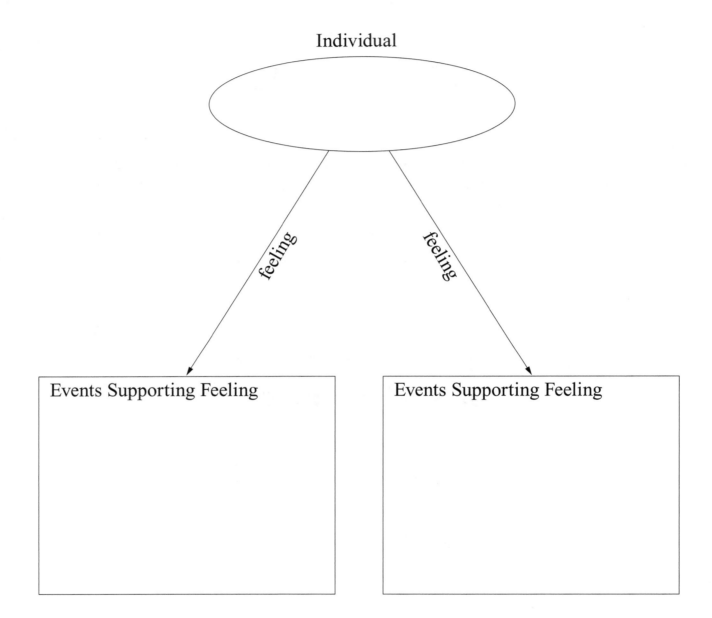

⊛ Character Feelings

Individual

feeling   feeling

Events Supporting Feeling   Events Supporting Feeling

Name _____ Date _____

◉★ Character Traits

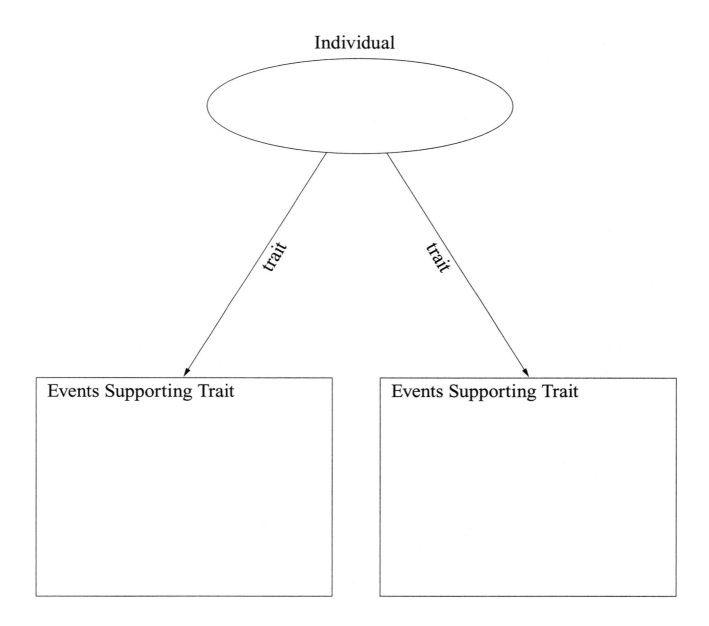

Individual

trait

trait

Events Supporting Trait

Events Supporting Trait

Concept Circles

FOCUS	TEXT	WHEN	WHY	HOW
✓Vocabulary	✓Narrative	Before Reading	Connecting ✓Questioning	✓Individual
✓Comprehension	✓Informational	During Reading	✓Synthesizing Inferring	✓Small Group
Response		✓After Reading	✓Determining Importance	Whole Group

DESCRIPTION

Concept Circles (Vacca & Vacca, 2002) provide opportunities for students to study words and relate them to one another. Concept Circles are intriguing to students as they categorize words in a visual way rather than in lists. This strategy is often viewed by students as "fun" while providing an opportunity for them to extend their understanding of concept words. There are three ways to work with Concept Circles. The first asks students to view a completed circle containing four words or phrases and to identify the concept represented by all of the words or phrases in the circle. In a second pattern, one or two of the quadrants are left empty and students are invited to add words to fit the concept as well as name it. The third way of using Concept Circles is to identify the word or phrase in the circle that does not relate to the others, shade it, and then identify the concept that exists among the remaining sections. Students could also be asked to replace the shaded word or phrase with one that fits the concept. All of the ways of working with Concept Circles involve students in thinking about how words relate to each other and how they relate to a superordinate concept. Concept Circles can serve as a quick and meaningful review of major concepts. Concept Circles also work well as an in-class activity, as a homework assignment, or as a means of assessing student understanding of major ideas and relationships.

Procedure

1. Make transparencies of the Concept Circles graphic organizers on pages 25–27 and display them on an overhead projector. Tell students that this type of graphic can help them think about some of the central concepts in their lesson or unit of study.

2. Model the use of Concept Circles by choosing well-understood concepts and inviting the class to participate in completing the circles with you. For example, the words in the circle might be *Dakota,*

Navigator, Escalade, and *RAV4.* Ask students, "What concept would include all of these words?" Students might suggest *automobiles, trucks,* or *sport utility vehicles.* Write the category they select on the line above the circle. Next, show another circle where the words included might be *steering wheel, visor, seats.* Ask, "What is the concept?" Students might say, "parts of cars" or "auto interiors." Write one of the responses on the line at the top of the Concept Circle on the transparency. Next ask, "What word could you add to our circle that fits the concept?" Students might suggest *seat belts, carpet,* or *odometer.* Choose one and write it in the blank quadrant of the circle. Finally, show students a completed circle in which one of the words included in the circle does not fit the concept. Have the students read the four words in the circle. Then ask them, "All but one relate to which concept?" An example might be *Ford, Chevrolet, Chrysler, Sony.* Then say, "One of the words doesn't belong. Can you identify it and tell us why you chose it?" After students identify *Sony* as the word that doesn't fit, shade in that quadrant with an overhead projector pen. Then ask students to identify the concept "cars" or "autos" and ask them to suggest a replacement for *Sony* that fits the concept. Students might suggest *Saturn* or *Toyota.* Write the new word in the quadrant.

3. After modeling, give students an opportunity to complete Concept Circles independently. You may want to invite students to work individually or in pairs to complete Concept Circle activities you have developed, or have them use the reproducible masters on pages 25–27 to create circles using words from the lesson or unit of study.

4. When the circles are completed, have students share some of their ideas or transfer them to a transparency and present them to the rest of the class. Their peers will enjoy matching wits with the circles' creators by guessing the superordinate concepts, suggesting other words that might relate to the concept, or reviewing the words that don't "fit" the identified concept.

Reference

Vacca, R. T., & Vacca, J. L. (2002). *Content area reading: Literacy and learning across the curriculum* (7th ed.). Boston: Allyn and Bacon.

Sample Concept Circles for Middle School Science Lesson on Geologic Time*

Concept Circles

Geologic Time
(topic)

✳ **DIRECTIONS**

Read the words in each circle. Determine the concept that includes all of the words or phrases in the circle. Write it on the line above the circle.

[Geologic Eras]

[Geologic Periods]

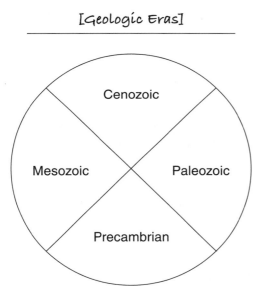

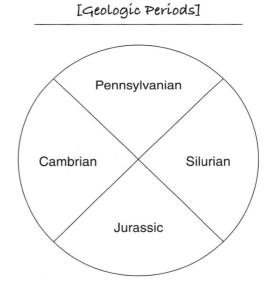

*Brackets [ ] indicate possible student responses.

✳ DIRECTIONS

Read the words in each circle. Think of a concept that includes the words in the circle and then add a word or phrase to the circle that fits the concept. Write the appropriate concept on the line above each circle.

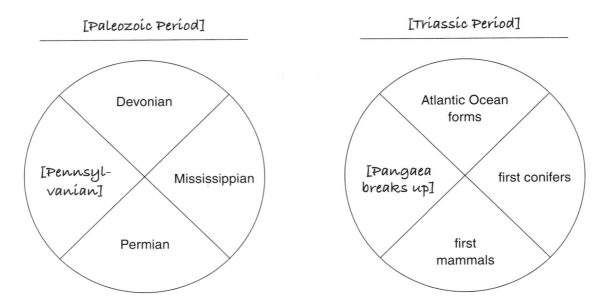

[Paleozoic Period]

Devonian

[Pennsyl-vanian]

Mississippian

Permian

[Triassic Period]

Atlantic Ocean forms

[Pangaea breaks up]

first conifers

first mammals

✳ DIRECTIONS

Read the words in each circle. Determine a concept that includes all but one of the words or phrases in the circle. Write the name of the concept on the line above the circle. Replace the word or phrase that doesn't fit with a better choice. Be prepared to defend your answers.

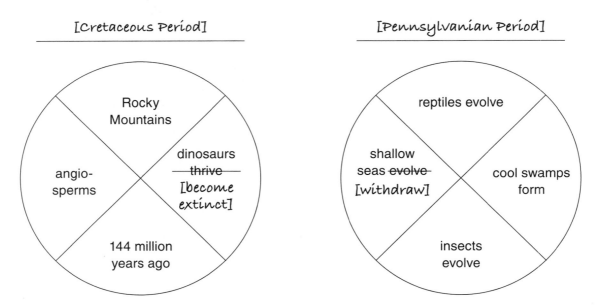

[Cretaceous Period]

Rocky Mountains

angio-sperms

dinosaurs ~~thrive~~ [become extinct]

144 million years ago

[Pennsylvanian Period]

reptiles evolve

shallow seas ~~evolve~~ [withdraw]

cool swamps form

insects evolve

---

*Brackets [ ] indicate possible student responses.

Name _____ Date _____

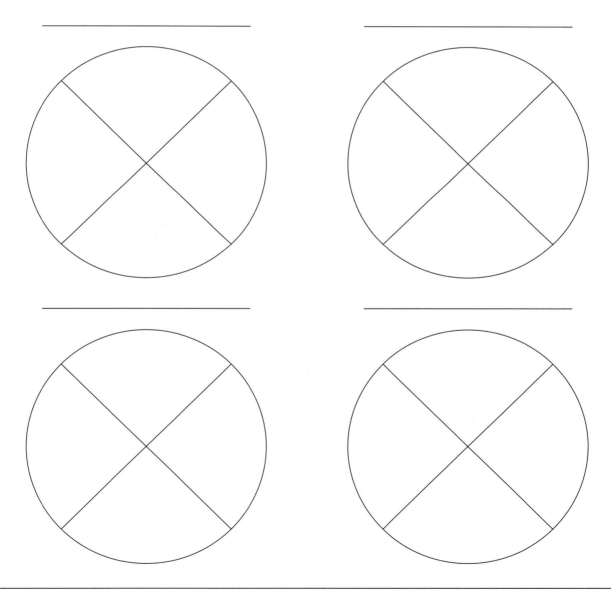

⬛⭐ Concept Circles

_____
(topic)

✳ DIRECTIONS

Read the words in each circle. Determine the concept that includes all of the words or phrases in the circle. Write it on the line above the circle.

Name _____ Date _____

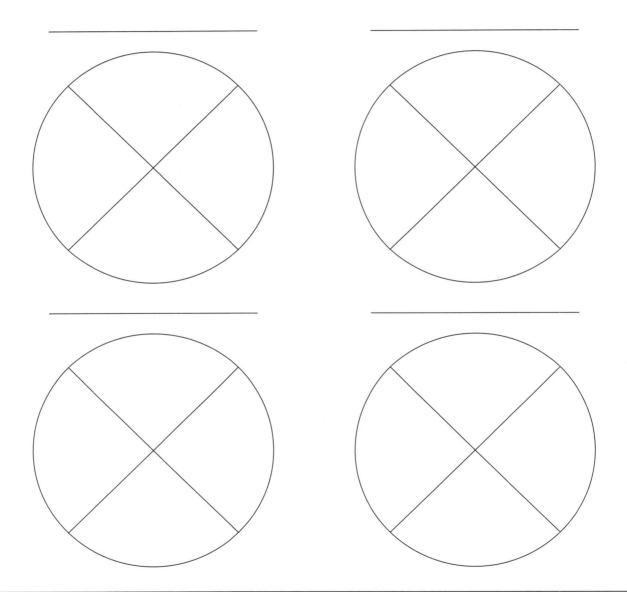

Concept Circles

_____
(topic)

☀ DIRECTIONS
Read the words in each circle. Think of a concept that includes the words in the circle and then add a word or phrase to the circle that fits the concept. Write the appropriate concept on the line above each circle.

Name _____ Date _____

Concept Circles

_____
(topic)

✳ **DIRECTIONS**

Read the words in each circle. Determine a concept that includes all but one of the words or phrases in the circle. Write the name of the concept on the line above the circle. Replace the word or phrase that doesn't fit with a better choice. Be prepared to defend your answers.

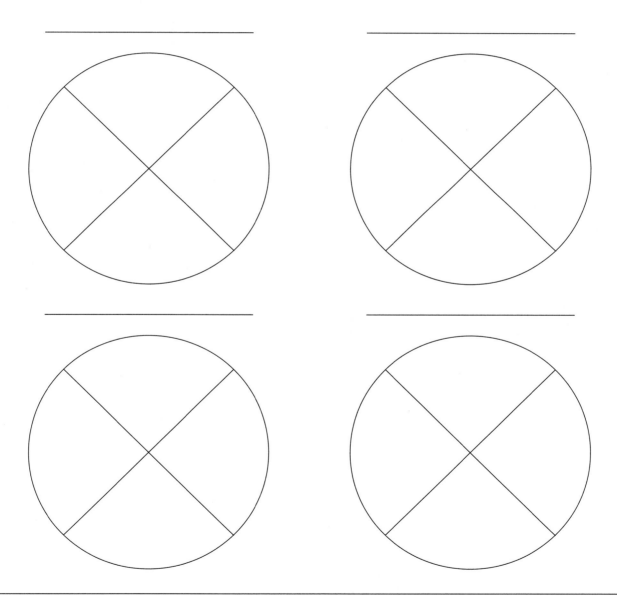

Concept Mapping

FOCUS	TEXT	WHEN	WHY	HOW
Vocabulary	✓Narrative	✓Before Reading	Connecting Questioning	✓Individual
✓Comprehension	✓Informational	✓During Reading	✓Synthesizing Inferring	✓Small Group
Response		✓After Reading	✓Determining Importance	✓Whole Group

DESCRIPTION

Concept Mapping (Novak, 1991) is a technique for visualizing relationships between concepts. Concept Maps are similar to semantic maps (Heimlich & Pittelman, 1986) in that they show the structure of information in graphic form. Concept Maps are diagrams that explicitly identify major and subordinate concepts of a topic and often include labels showing how the concepts are related. Concept Maps are most often used with informational text, are especially useful in science, and are often individually designed to fit the ideas. They can be used as an advance organizer before reading to help students understand the structure of the information they will be studying. Concept Maps can also be used as a study and note-taking guide during reading where students are provided with the major concepts and asked to identify and map the related subordinate concepts as they read. Most often, however, Concept Maps are used at the culmination of a unit of study to show, in a graphic way, a synthesis of the information that has been learned. Concept Maps can be useful study tools for students and can also be used as means of assessing student learning (Rafferty & Fleschner, 1993).

Procedure

1. Identify the major concepts of the topic being studied and select an appropriate Concept Map from pages 32–34, the CD-ROM, or create one to fit your purposes.
2. Make an overhead transparency or enlarged version of the map.
3. Provide copies of the map to students.
4. Explain to students that they are going to be developing Concept Maps in order to review their work with a specific topic or subject, for example, in a study of the Digestive System, the function of the stomach.

5. Write Stomach Wall in the box at the top of the Hierarchy Concept Map and invite students to do the same on their maps.

6. Ask students to review the text information related to the topic and suggest the major concepts that they believe should be included on the map. Often, chapter headings and subheadings can be used to generate the list.

7. Next, work with students to organize the list from the most general or abstract to the most specific.

8. From the list, select the major concepts and have students write them in the appropriate spaces on the Concept Map.

9. Invite students to work individually or in pairs to add details to one or more of the central concepts on the map.

10. After students have finished their work, have them share the information from their maps and add the ideas to the enlarged map.

11. Review with students how the concepts are connected and the relationships among the ideas represented on the Concept Maps. Remind them that they can use their maps to help them remember and use the information in the chapter or unit.

An additional reproducible can be found on the CD-ROM accompanying this book.

References

Heimlich, J. E., & Pittelman, S. D. (1986). *Semantic mapping: Classroom applications.* Newark, DE: International Reading Association.

Novak, J. D. (1991). Classify with concept maps: A tool for students and teachers alike. *The Science Teacher, 58,* 45–49.

Rafferty, C. D., & Fleschner, L. K. (1993). Concept mapping: A viable alternative to objective essay exams. *Reading Research Quarterly, 32,* 25–34.

Sample Hierarchy Concept Map for **Science**

Digestion in Stomach

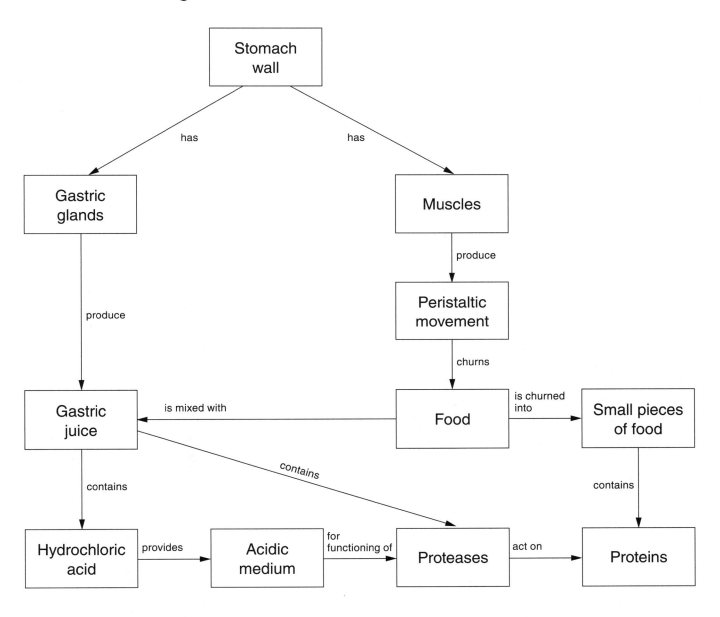

Name _____ Date _____

⬟ ★ Hierarchy Concept Map

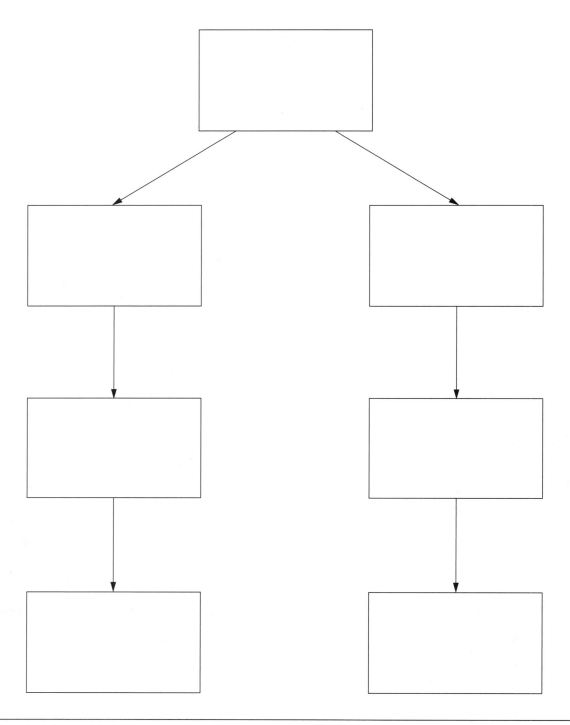

⊛ Spider Concept Map

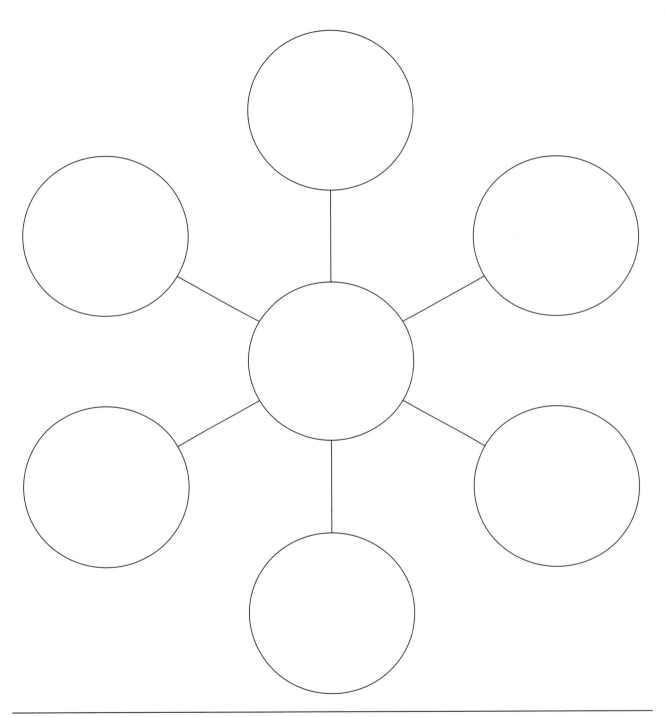

⬛⭐ Flow Chart Concept Map

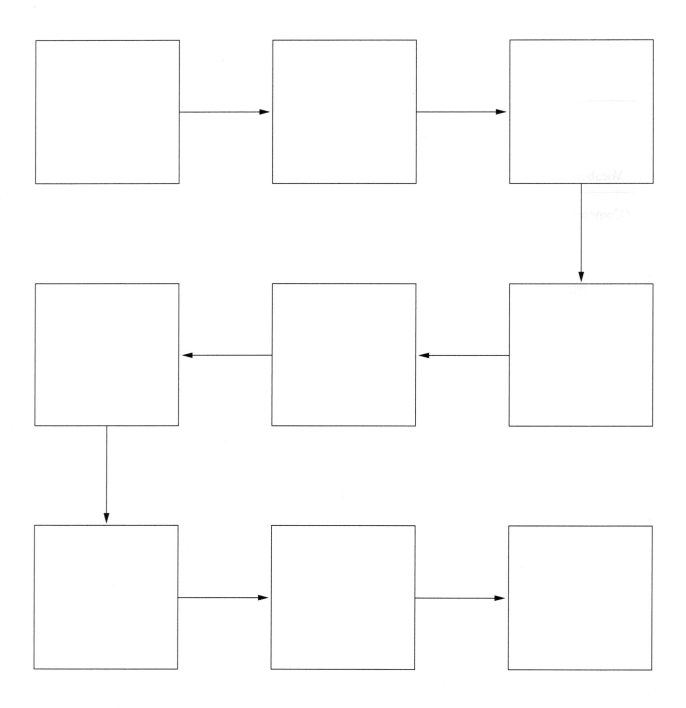

Discussion Web

FOCUS	TEXT	WHEN	WHY		HOW
Vocabulary	✓Narrative	Before Reading	Connecting	Questioning	Individual
✓Comprehension	✓Informational	During Reading	✓Synthesizing	✓Inferring	✓Small Group
✓Response		✓After Reading	✓Determining Importance		✓Whole Group

DESCRIPTION

The Discussion Web (Alvermann, 1991; Duthie, 1986) is a graphic aid for helping students address both sides of an issue by considering pro and con arguments before drawing a conclusion. Active discussion is stimulated by this strategy, which incorporates reading, speaking, listening, and writing.

Procedure

1. Choose a selection that has the potential to generate opposing viewpoints. Be sure to initially develop an understanding of key vocabulary, survey illustrations and charts, build background knowledge as needed, and help students set purposes for reading. Then have students read the selection.

2. Make an overhead transparency of the reproducible master on page 39 and duplicate and distribute copies to students. Use the transparency on the overhead projector to introduce the Discussion Web. Pose a question related to the selection that stimulates opposing views and have students write the question on their Discussion Web.

3. Have students work with a partner to brainstorm at least three responses for each side of the question posed. Encourage students to write down key words or phrases and strive to have an equal number of reasons in each column. Students could take turns writing reasons on the same Discussion Web. Provide ample time for each set of partners to share their reasons.

4. Pair one set of partners with another set of partners so they can compare their reasons. Tell the groups that the goal is to work toward consensus. Provide time for students to share and discuss. Encourage students to listen carefully, especially for views that may differ from their own. The conclusion can be written in the box on the bottom of the sheet.

5. Select or have each group select an individual to serve as a group spokesperson. Provide three to five minutes for each group to decide which of the group's reasons best support the group's conclusion and check or star the best reasons. Then have the spokesperson from each group report to the whole class.

6. If desired, invite students to write their individual answers to the question posed on the Discussion Web.

7. Consider the following variations of the Discussion Web based on Alvermann (1991) and Swafford (1990).

   • Current or historical issues can be explored by making simple changes in the Discussion Web. The U.S. Civil War slavery issue could be examined through the positions of Stephen A. Douglas and Abraham Lincoln. A partial Discussion Web showing this example follows.

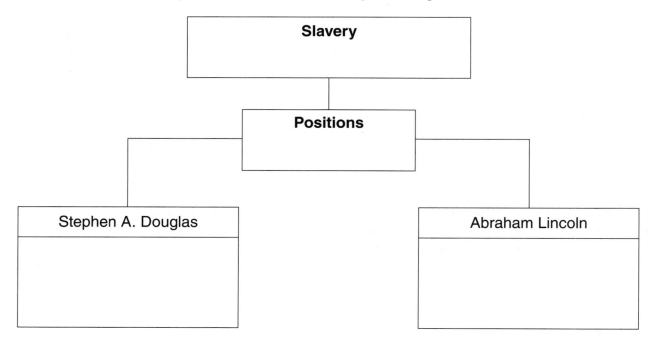

   • Before reading a selection, adapt the Discussion Web to stimulate the students' predictions. In the short story titled "Cheating Mr. Diskin," students could complete a Discussion Web adapted as follows.

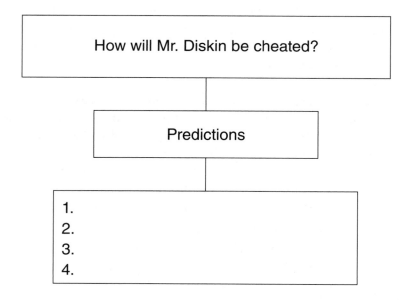

The story could be read to see which, if any, of the predictions are supported.

- For word problems in mathematics, students can be asked to classify the information from the word problems as relevant or irrelevant in an effort to focus on what is necessary to solve the problem. An example is shown below.

Hem was 12. Scott was 13. Carlos was also 13. The three boys reported their classes' results for the food drive. Hem's class collected 27 items. Scott's class collected 32 items, and Carlos' class collected 39 items. What was the average number of items collected for the food drive?

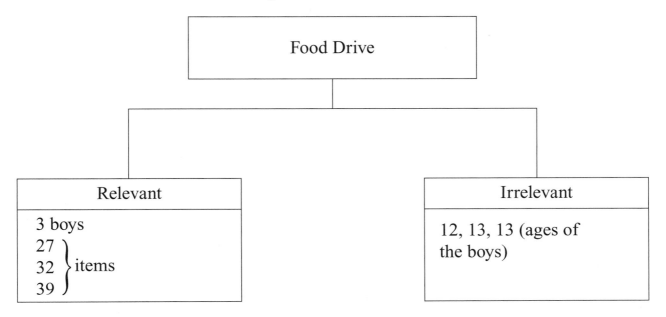

References

Alvermann, D. (1991). The discussion web: A graphic aid for learning across the curriculum. *The Reading Teacher, 45,* 92–99.

Duthie, J. (1986). The web: A powerful tool for the teaching and evaluation of the expository essay. *The History and Social Studies Teacher, 21,* 232–236.

Swafford, J. (1990, July). *Discussion strategies for improving reading and writing to learn.* Paper presented at the World Congress on Reading, Stockholm, Sweden.

Sample Discussion Web
for **Social Studies**

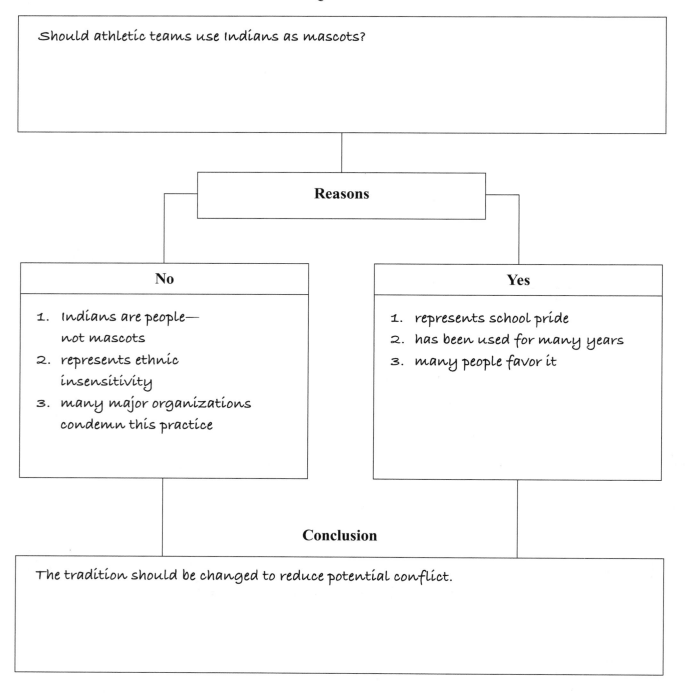

Question

Should athletic teams use Indians as mascots?

Reasons

No

1. Indians are people—not mascots
2. represents ethnic insensitivity
3. many major organizations condemn this practice

Yes

1. represents school pride
2. has been used for many years
3. many people favor it

Conclusion

The tradition should be changed to reduce potential conflict.

Name _____ Date _____

⊛ Discussion Web

Question

Reasons

No	**Yes**

Conclusion

Double-Entry Journal

FOCUS	TEXT	WHEN	WHY		HOW
Vocabulary	✓Narrative	Before Reading	✓Connecting	✓Questioning	✓Individual
✓Comprehension	✓Informational	✓During Reading	✓Synthesizing	✓Inferring	✓Small Group
✓Response		After Reading	✓Determining Importance		Whole Group

DESCRIPTION

Double-Entry Journals (Tovani, 2000) are a form of guided note taking that help students track their thinking and interact with text while reading. Similar in format to two-column notes, Double-Entry Journals are more flexible and allow students to respond to their reading in a variety of ways. For example, by making connections, noting confusing parts, listing interesting facts or details, drawing a sketch, or noting a difficult vocabulary word, students can respond to their reading and expand their thinking.

Procedure

1. Have students fold a piece of paper in half lengthwise or provide copies of one of the Double-Entry Journal reproducibles on pages 44–46 or on the CD-ROM.

2. Explain to students that on the left side of the paper, they will copy sentences or words from the text, noting the page(s) where they can be found.

3. On the right side of the paper, students should write their thinking related to the ideas they have written on the left side of the paper. For example, you might say the following.

   Today I am going to read a section of our current events newspaper aloud and show you how I track my thinking as I read by using my Double-Entry Journal. There are several ways that I could respond to the reading, but today I am going to use, "I wonder . . ." to focus my thinking.

4. Read a section of the text aloud. As you read, write down a quotation or word that you have a question about. For example, you might say the following.

   In our text it says that 300 million Africans lack access to safe water. On the left side of my paper I am going to write, "Bad water" and note that it is discussed on page 8.

   On the right side of my paper I am going to write, "I wonder what caused the problem?"

5. Continue modeling your note taking and I Wonder questions until you think that students understand how to proceed.

6. Invite students to work individually or in pairs to read the remainder of the selection and create notes and questions using their Double-Entry Journals.

7. When students have completed the reading, invite them to read their quotations and questions and use them as a basis for a class discussion of the reading.

8. Tovani (2000) suggests starting with one response prompt and providing practice opportunities for students before introducing additional response options for use in the Double-Entry Journals.

Additional reproducibles can be found on the CD-ROM accompanying this book.

Reference

Tovani, C. (2000). *I read it, but I don't get it: Comprehension strategies for adolescent readers.* Portland, ME: Stenhouse.

⊛ Double-Entry Journal

WHAT THE TEXT SAYS	WHAT I WONDER
1. Bad water—300 million Africans lack access to safe water. Page 1	1. I wonder what caused the problem?
2. Government doesn't work. Page 3	2. I wonder what the government of Malawi is like? I wonder why they don't do something?
3. The best solutions come from sitting down as close to the problem as possible and talking with the people. Page 4	3. I wonder if this isn't the best way to solve most problems?
4. Cell phones, e-mail, and migrants are connecting Africa with urban America. Page 5	4. I wonder how Africans get the cell phones when they can't get to fresh water?
5. Water for People is making a difference. Page 6	5. I wonder how we could help this cause? I wonder if our Student Council could sponsor this?

Name _____ Date _____

Selection _____

⊕ Double-Entry Journal

WHAT THE TEXT SAYS	WHAT I WONDER
1. Page ____	1.
2. Page ____	2.
3. Page ____	3.
4. Page ____	4.
5. Page ____	5.

Name _____ Date _____

Selection

★ Double-Entry Journal

WHAT THE TEXT SAYS	WHAT I THINK
1. Page ____	**1.**
2. Page ____	**2.**
3. Page ____	**3.**
4. Page ____	**4.**
5. Page ____	**5.**

Name _____ Date _____

Selection _____

⊛ Double-Entry Journal

WHAT THE TEXT SAYS	WHY IT'S IMPORTANT
1. Page ____	1.
2. Page ____	2.
3. Page ____	3.
4. Page ____	4.
5. Page ____	5.

Exit Slips

FOCUS	TEXT	WHEN	WHY	HOW
Vocabulary	✓Narrative	Before Reading	Connecting ✓Questioning	✓Individual
Comprehension	✓Informational	During Reading	✓Synthesizing Inferring	Small Group
✓Response		✓After Reading	Determining Importance	Whole Group

DESCRIPTION

Exit Slips (Lenski & Johns, 2004; Short, Harste, & Burke, 1996) are quick ways to invite student response after learning. Exit slips are completed at the end of a class period and are generally collected by the teacher as students leave the room. Exit slips provide quick feedback for the teacher about how well students understood the lesson and what might need to be addressed in a future lesson.

Procedure

1. Consider the type of response you wish to receive from your students.
2. Make a copy of one of the Exit Slip reproducible masters on pages 49–52. Choose the statement(s) to which you want the students to respond. Make a copy for each student.
3. After your lesson, distribute the slips and direct students to respond to one or two of the phrases you have chosen. Be focused and selective in the phrases you choose.
4. As students leave the classroom or at the end of the lesson, collect the slips. Use them to assess student response to learning and plan follow-up instruction.

References

Lenski, S. D., & Johns, J. L. (2004). *Improving writing: K–8 Strategies, assessments, and resources* (2nd ed.). Dubuque, IA: Kendall/Hunt.

Short, K. G., Harste, J. C., & Burke, C. (1996). *Creating classrooms for authors and inquirers* (2nd ed.). Portsmouth, NH: Heinemann.

Sample Exit Slip
for Middle School **Geography**

✳ DIRECTIONS

Please respond to one or more of the statements below as directed by your teacher.

1. Today I learned . . .

2. I don't understand . . .

3. I would like to learn more about . . . *whether global warming is really a problem and how it might affect me.*

4. A question I have is . . .

5. Please explain more about . . .

6. The most important thing I learned today is . . .

7. Three things I learned today are . . .

8. The thing that surprised me most today was . . .

9. I wish . . . *we could work with our partners more often in class.*

10. The best part of class today was . . .

Name _____ Date _____

⊛ Exit Slip

✳ DIRECTIONS

Please respond to one or more of the statements below as directed by your teacher.

1. Today I learned . . .

2. I don't understand . . .

3. I would like to learn more about . . .

4. A question I have is . . .

5. Please explain more about . . .

6. The most important thing I learned today is . . .

7. Three things I learned today are . . .

8. The thing that surprised me most today was . . .

9. I wish . . .

10. The best part of class today was . . .

Name _____ Date _____

Exit Slip

3 Things I Learned

_____
_____
_____

2 Things I Found Interesting

_____
_____

1 Question I Still Have

_____
_____

Name _____ Date _____

Exit Slip

3 Things I Learned

_____
_____
_____

2 Things I Found Interesting

_____
_____

1 Question I Still Have

_____
_____

Name _____ Date _____

Exit Slip

3 Things I Learned

_____
_____
_____

2 Things I Found Interesting

_____
_____

1 Question I Still Have

_____
_____

Name _____ Date _____

Subject _____ Period _____

Vocabulary Exit Slip

Three words I learned today are:

a) _____ b) _____ c) _____

Here is one of the words in a sentence:

_____

_____

_____

Name _____ Date _____

Subject _____ Period _____

Vocabulary Exit Slip

Three words I learned today are:

a) _____ b) _____ c) _____

Here is one of the words in a sentence:

_____

_____

_____

Name _____ Date _____

Subject _____ Period _____

Vocabulary Exit Slip

Three words I learned today are:

a) _____ b) _____ c) _____

Here is one of the words in a sentence:

_____

_____

_____

Name _____ Date _____

Subject _____ Period _____

Exit Slip

Today I learned that:

_____

_____

_____

It is important because:

_____

_____

_____

Name _____ Date _____

Subject _____ Period _____

Exit Slip

Today I learned that:

_____

_____

_____

It is important because:

_____

_____

_____

Name _____ Date _____

Subject _____ Period _____

Exit Slip

Today I learned that:

_____

_____

_____

It is important because:

_____

_____

_____

Four Square

FOCUS	TEXT	WHEN	WHY		HOW
✓Vocabulary	✓Narrative	✓Before Reading	✓Connecting	Questioning	✓Individual
Comprehension	✓Informational	During Reading	Synthesizing	Inferring	✓Small Group
Response		✓After Reading	Determining Importance		✓Whole Group

DESCRIPTION

Four Square (Lenski, Wham, Johns, & Caskey, 2006) is an easy-to-use strategy that helps students learn meanings for new words. Because students are asked to make personal associations with the new word, word learning and retention may be enhanced.

Procedure

1. Make an overhead transparency of the reproducible master on page 56 or draw a square with four quadrants on the board. Label them as shown in the example below.

Word	Personal Clue or Connection
Definition	Opposite

2. Tell students that you are sharing a strategy that will help them learn and remember important vocabulary words. Then write a vocabulary word in the upper-left quadrant. Invite a student to pronounce the word.

3. Ask students to offer words or phrases that they personally associate with the vocabulary word. Write one of their associations in the upper-right quadrant. An alternative for words may be a picture or logo that is drawn in one of the quadrants.

4. Invite a student who may know the meaning of the word to offer it. Encourage other students to react to the definition and provide clarification as needed. Then write a brief definition of the word in the lower-left quadrant.

5. Have students offer words or phrases that are opposite in meaning. Discuss the responses and select a word or phrase to write in the lower-right quadrant.

6. Give students copies made from the Four Square reproducible master on page 56. Provide words from a reading selection for students to use. Have students work individually to complete their squares. Then provide time for students to discuss their squares in groups of three to five students.

7. Clarify the meanings of the words selected with the whole group.

8. Have students use the Four Square strategy independently with words you believe to be important in understanding the content of your lesson or unit of study.

Reference

Lenski, S. D., Wham, M. A., Johns, J. L., & Caskey, M. M. (2006). *Reading and learning strategies: Middle grades through high school* (3rd ed.). Dubuque, IA: Kendall/Hunt.

Sample of Four Square
for **Science**

Word	Personal Clue or Connection
electrolysis	chlorine is made from electrolysis and put in our drinking water
Definition	**Opposite**
electrical energy is used to bring about a change	corrosion—solutions transfer electrons and break down metals

Sample of Four Square
for **Social Studies**

Word	Personal Clue or Connection
stifle	to dampen the spirit
Definition	**Opposite**
to smother to prevent	enable

Name _____ Date _____

 **Four Square**

Word	Personal Clue or Connection
Definition	**Opposite**

Word	Personal Clue or Connection
Definition	**Opposite**

Frayer Model

FOCUS	TEXT	WHEN	WHY	HOW
✓Vocabulary	✓Narrative	✓Before Reading	Connecting Questioning	Individual
Comprehension	✓Informational	During Reading	✓Synthesizing Inferring	✓Small Group
Response		✓After Reading	✓Determining Importance	✓Whole Group

DESCRIPTION

The Frayer Model (Frayer, Fredrick, & Klausmeier, 1969) is a categorization activity that helps students develop a thorough understanding of important concepts. It also provides a visual means of distinguishing items that help define the concept from those that are merely associated with it.

Procedure

1. Using the reproducible master on page 61, make a transparency for use in the lesson.
2. Select a key word or concept from the lesson, for example, *ecosystem.*
3. Generate a list of key characteristics of the concept. Key characteristics for *ecosystem* might be *relationships, interactions, surroundings, living things,* and *nonliving things.*
4. Introduce the concept to students and show them your list of the key characteristics. Using the reproducible master on page 61, make copies for the students. In small cooperative groups, have students generate examples of the concept. Record responses on the Frayer Model graphic organizer. Examples of ecosystems might be *forests, cities, deserts,* and *oceans.*
5. Have students read the selection and check to see if the characteristics and examples are accurate. Take time to clarify meaning for nonessential characteristics and nonexamples.
6. Have students add nonessential characteristics and nonexamples of the concept to their organizer. Some items from their original list of characteristics and examples may need to be moved to other sections of the model based on their reading and collaborating with their peers. Depending on the specific ecosystem under consideration, nonessential characteristics of an ecosystem might be *glaciers, insects, buildings,* or *birds.* Nonexamples of an ecosystem might be *automobiles, solutions,* or *electricity.*

7. Once students are secure in the essential and nonessential characteristics as well as examples and nonexamples of the concept, have them relate the concept to a subordinate concept, a superordinate concept, and, finally, a coordinate term. For example, a subordinate concept for ecosystem might be *habitat*. A superordinate concept might be *environment*. A similar or coordinate phrase might be *community of organisms*.

An additional reproducible master can be found on the CD-ROM accompanying this book.

Reference

Frayer, D. A., Fredrick, W. C., & Klausmeier, H. J. (1969). *A schema for testing the level of concept mastery: Report from the project on situational variables and efficiency of concept learning.* Madison, WI: Wisconsin Research and Development Center for Cognitive Learning.

Sample Frayer Model
for **Biology**

Essential Characteristics	Nonessential Characteristics
Have organized nuclei Flagella or cilia Unicellular Microscopic Live in water or damp places	Contain chlorophyll Sexual Asexual Capture food

PROTIST

Examples	Nonexamples
Euglena Diatoms Protozoa Slime molds Paramecia	Animals Fungi Plants Monerans

A word that means about the same as protist is _____protista_____.

A word that is more general than protist is _____organism_____.

A word that is more specific than protist is _____protozoa_____.

Sample Frayer Model
for **Math**

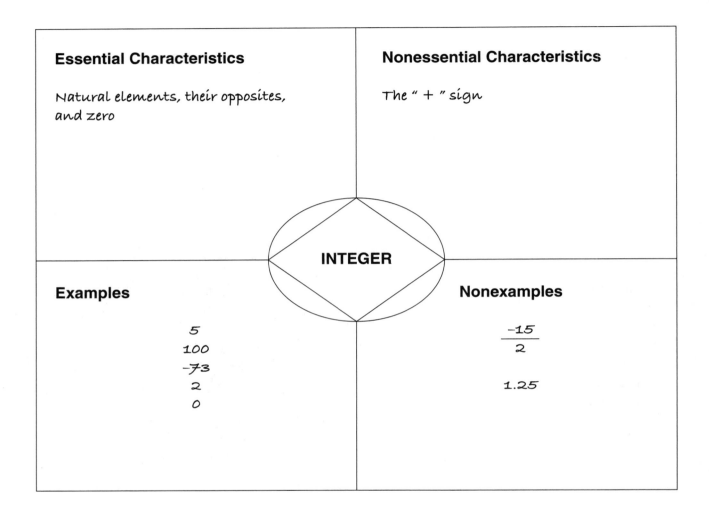

Essential Characteristics

Natural elements, their opposites, and zero

Nonessential Characteristics

The " + " sign

INTEGER

Examples

5
100
−73
2
0

Nonexamples

$\dfrac{-15}{2}$

1.25

A word that means about the same as integer is _____signed number_____ .

A word that is more general than integer is _____rational number_____ .

A word that is more specific than integer is _____whole number_____ .

⊛ **Frayer Model**

Essential Characteristics	Nonessential Characteristics
Examples	Nonexamples

A word that means about the same as the key term is _____ .

A word that is more general than the key term is _____ .

A word that is more specific than the key term is _____ .

Info Boxes

FOCUS	TEXT	WHEN	WHY	HOW
✓Vocabulary	✓Narrative	Before Reading	Connecting Questioning	✓Individual
✓Comprehension	✓Informational	During Reading	Synthesizing Inferring	✓Small Group
Response		✓After Reading	✓Determining Importance	✓Whole Group

DESCRIPTION

Info Boxes (adapted from Allen, 2000; Beers, 2003; and Hoyt, 1999;) provide a way for students to recall and organize information about a chapter or topic after reading or learning about it. The completed grid can be used to stimulate discussion, determine main ideas and details, and create summaries. Completed grids can also be used as information sources for more extended writing projects.

Procedure

1. Create a grid containing one or more letters of the alphabet in each box of the grid or use one of the graphic organizers on pages 66–67 or on the CD-ROM.
2. Write the topic or title at the top of the grid and duplicate copies for students.
3. At the completion of a chapter or unit of study, distribute copies of the grid to students. You might say the following.

    We have been studying pond scum. Think about the information we have gained through our text reading, our internet research, our laboratory work, and our visit to Coal Creek. Work with your laboratory partner and try to record one or more ideas in each box of the grid. Each of the ideas in the grid must start with the letter or one of the letters of the alphabet that are written in the grid.

4. When students have completed the task, say the following.

    Look at the grid of information you have developed. Review the information with your partner. Decide which ideas in the grid are the most important and circle them.

5. When students have determined the most important information, encourage them to write a summary and share it orally with the class.

6. Students may also use the ideas in the grid as a basis for developing a longer piece of writing on the topic.

7. Info Boxes are also excellent resources for use in review and test preparation.

An additional reproducible can be found on the CD-ROM accompanying this book.

References

Allen, J. (2000). *Yellow brick roads: Shared and guided paths to independent reading 4–12*. Portland, ME: Stenhouse.

Beers, K. (2003). *When kids can't read, what teachers can do*. Portsmouth, NH: Heinemann.

Hoyt, L. (1999). *Revisit, reflect, retell: Strategies for improving reading comprehension*. Portsmouth, NH: Heinemann.

Sample Info Boxes
for **Biology**

Name _____Jenny and Emily_____ Date ___October 10___

Title/Subject _____The Promise of Pond Scum_____

A Alga can produce hydrogen After photosynthesis process	**B**	**C** Convert solar energy directly into hydrogen (electricity) Coal alternative	**D** Depleted fossil fuels
E Enzymes	**F** Fuel consumption growing	**G** Golden, Colorado Green algae Gluttonous demand for power Gas alternative	**H** Hydrogenase enzymes
I	**J**	**K**	**L** Living organisms
M Manipulate photosynthesis Microbes	**N** National Renewable Energy Lab	**O**	**P** Photosynthesis-to-hydrogen process Photovoltaics expensive and inefficient Photosynthesis original source of fossil fuels
Q	**R** Resources depleted	**S** Sunlight needed for photosynthesis	**T** Turn solar rays into molecular energy Twenty million barrels of oil a day
U	**V**	**W** Withhold sulfate	**XYZ**

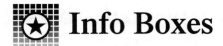 **Info Boxes**

Name _____ Date _____

Title/Subject _____

A	B	C	D
E	F	G	H
I	J	K	L
M	N	O	P
Q	R	S	T
U	V	W	XYZ

 **Info Boxes**

Name _____ Date _____

Title/Subject _____

AB	**CD**	**EF**	**GH**
IJ	**KL**	**MN**	**OP**
QRS	**TU**	**VW**	**XYZ**

Summary: _____

_____

_____

_____

_____

_____

_____

Intra-Act

FOCUS	TEXT	WHEN	WHY	HOW
Vocabulary	✓Narrative	Before Reading	✓Connecting ✓Questioning	✓Individual
✓Comprehension	✓Informational	During Reading	✓Synthesizing ✓Inferring	✓Small Group
Response		✓After Reading	Determining Importance	✓Whole Group

DESCRIPTION

The Intra-Act strategy (Hoffman, 1979) encourages students to construct their own decisions about issues by making intertextual links. In four steps, students move from first formulating opinions based solely upon one text to ultimately basing their opinions upon further research, group discussions, and reflection. The four steps are: 1) students construct meaning from a text selection; 2) students make connections between the information in the first text and other resources they find on the topic; 3) students share their own feelings on the topic and the values those feelings convey; and 4) students reflect on the newly formed values.

Procedure

1. Make an overhead transparency and duplicate copies of the Intra-Act reproducible master on page 72 or adapt it to suit your needs or purposes.

2. Explain to students the difference between topics that are explanatory, such as how a bill becomes a law, and topics that are subject to opinion, such as whether certain bills should become laws.

3. Use the sample topic and chart on page 71 or develop an example from your curriculum to demonstrate to students how the Intra-Act strategy works. Show examples of statements to the students. Brainstorm with students other statements that could be made to stimulate debate on the sample topic.

4. Either on your own or with students' input, choose another controversial topic for which you can find several sources. The topic should be one that readily lends itself to differing opinions.

5. Assign the first reading on the controversial topic. Following the reading, brainstorm with students possible opinion statements that can be made about the reading. It should be possible to answer the

statements with either yes or no. Choose four of the statements and write them under *Statements* on the reproducible master. Duplicate copies of the master for students.

6. Assign students to work in small heterogeneous groups (3 to 4 students per group). The groups should take seven to ten minutes to summarize and discuss the reading. Assign a leader in each group to write or report the summary of the reading.

7. Allow students class time to research their topics using other literature and media. You may wish to enlist the help of your school's librarian or media specialist to provide a wide variety of relevant material for your classroom. Instruct students to be prepared to share and discuss their findings in their next group meeting.

8. Schedule time for students to meet in their small groups to compare their research findings and any conclusions they have drawn about the topic.

9. After students have explored the topic more thoroughly, they will begin the valuative phase of the discussion. In this phase, students work independently. First, students fill in the names of each of their group members across the top row of the grid. Next, they write yes or no under their own name in response to each statement. Finally, they predict how each member of their group will respond to the statements and write yes or no under each member's names after each statement.

10. Students meet again with their groups and share their responses to the statements. As each student shares, the other group members compare the student's responses to their predictions.

11. Finally, open the discussion to the whole class. Encourage students to share the reasons for their responses, and allow opportunities to challenge, support, and question one another. This is an opportune time to reinforce student skills of offering constructive criticism and disagreeing respectfully and assertively, not aggressively.

Reference

Hoffman, J. V. (1979). The intra-act procedure for critical reading. *Journal of Reading, 22,* 605–608.

Sample of Intra-Act
for **Social Studies**

Topic: Was it appropriate for the United States to enter into the Iraq War?

(Write group members' names, including your own, in the top row of blanks.)

Statements	José	Anna	Tom	Xiao Peng
The U.S. has an obligation to enforce justice and world peace.				
We had no business being across the world in someone else's fight.				
We (the U.S.) were the best candidates to eliminate Saddam Hussein.				
We should have spent all the money that was spent on the Iraq War on our public schools instead.				

❋ DIRECTIONS

1. Think about the above statements and then under your name write *yes* if you agree with the statement or *no* if you disagree with the statement.

2. Under each group member's name, predict how that person will respond to the statements by writing *yes* or *no* by each statement under the name.

3. When you meet with your group, compare your predictions to how members really answered.

4. When the class meets to discuss the statements, use the information you found in your research to help you challenge, support, or question your own and others' opinions. Remember to listen well, support your responses with your research, and be respectful to others in your responses.

Name _____ Date _____

 **Intra-Act**

Topic: _____

(Write group members' names, including your own, in the top row of blanks.)

Statements				

✳ DIRECTIONS

1. Think about the above statements and then under your name write *yes* if you agree with the statement or *no* if you disagree with the statement.

2. Under each member's name, predict how that person will respond to the statements by writing *yes* or *no* by each statement under the name.

3. When you meet with your group, compare your predictions to how members really answered.

4. When the class meets to discuss the statements, use the information you found in your research to help you challenge, support, or question your own and others' opinions. Remember to listen well, support your responses with your research, and be respectful to others in your responses.

Knowledge Rating

FOCUS	TEXT	WHEN	WHY	HOW
✓Vocabulary	✓Narrative	✓Before Reading	✓Connecting Questioning	✓Individual
Comprehension	✓Informational	During Reading	Synthesizing Inferring	✓Small Group
Response		After Reading	Determining Importance	Whole Group

DESCRIPTION

Knowledge Rating (Blachowicz, 1986; Blachowicz & Fisher, 2006) is a prereading activity that encourages students to develop sensitivity to and awareness of words by responding to a list of words that reflects the content of the lesson. This self-evaluation strategy serves to activate prior knowledge and helps students to make predictions about what is to be learned. Using the Knowledge Rating sheet and participating in related discussion helps students understand that word meanings evolve with use and experience. A deepening understanding of words evolves over time.

Procedure

1. Select several vocabulary words that reflect the content of the lesson.
2. Write these words on one of the Knowledge Rating reproducible masters on pages 75–76. Duplicate and distribute it to students or have students copy the words from the overhead projector or board.
3. Invite students to rate their knowledge of each word according to one of the following categories: 1) Know It Well, 2) Think I Know It, 3) Have Heard/Seen It, and 4) No Clue.
4. Divide your class into small heterogeneous groups and invite students to discuss their knowledge of each word. Invite students to define those words that fall into the *Know It Well* category.
5. Circulate through the classroom while students are discussing the words. Listen to students' comments to determine their knowledge about the subject.
6. Have the small heterogeneous groups return to a whole group setting. Conduct a brief discussion of the words, focusing on particular meanings or features that are appropriate. Invite the students to make predictions about the content of the lesson, based on their expanding knowledge of some of the words contained in it. For example, you might say, "Looking at these words, what do you think we might find out about in this lesson?"

7. Record students' ideas on an overhead transparency or on the board.

8. Invite students to participate in the lesson, be aware of the words as they are encountered, and determine if their predictions were correct. If the words are from a reading selection, encourage students to use the context to help clarify word meanings.

> Additional examples can be found on the CD-ROM accompanying this book.

Sample Knowledge Rating for High School Math

✳ DIRECTIONS

Below are some words that you will find in your lesson. Rate your knowledge for each of the words by placing a ✓ under the category you have chosen.

WORD	(1) KNOW IT WELL	(2) THINK I KNOW IT	(3) HAVE HEARD/ SEEN IT	(4) NO CLUE
intercepts		✓		
x-axis			✓	
zero	✓			
vertex				✓
symmetry				✓
maximum	✓			
minimum	✓			

References

Blachowicz, C. L. Z. (1986). Making connections: Alternatives to the vocabulary notebook. *Journal of Reading, 29,* 643–649.

Blachowicz, C., & Fisher, P. (2006). *Teaching vocabulary in all classrooms* (3rd ed.). Upper Saddle River, NJ: Pearson.

Name _____ Date _____

 **Knowledge Rating**

❋ DIRECTIONS

Below are some words that you will find in your lesson. Rate your knowledge for each of the words by placing an X under the category you have chosen.

WORD	(1) KNOW IT WELL	(2) THINK I KNOW IT	(3) HAVE HEARD/ SEEN IT	(4) NO CLUE

Name _____ Date _____

◉ Knowledge Rating

✳ Before, During, and After Reading

DIRECTIONS

Read the words. If you know the meaning before reading, write the definition and place a plus (+) in the "Before Reading" column. Use a minus (–) if you don't know the meaning and a question mark (?) if you are unsure. During reading, try to determine the meanings for unknown words from any clues in the passage. Use the –, +, and ? symbols. If the meaning is clear, write it. After discussion, use the symbols to rate any words whose meanings were not already listed or clarified. Write meanings for any remaining words by consulting appropriate reference sources.

WORD	BEFORE READING	DURING READING	AFTER DISCUSSION	WORD'S MEANING
1.				
2.				
3.				
4.				
5.				
6.				
7.				
8.				
9.				
10.				

Know-Want-Learned Plus
(K-W-L Plus)

FOCUS	TEXT	WHEN	WHY	HOW
Vocabulary	✓Narrative	✓Before Reading	✓Connecting ✓Questioning	✓Individual
✓Comprehension	✓Informational	During Reading	✓Synthesizing ✓Inferring	✓Small Group
✓Response		✓After Reading	✓Determining Importance	✓Whole Group

DESCRIPTION

The K-W-L Plus strategy stimulates students' background knowledge before learning and organizes their knowledge after learning. The K-W-L strategy was originally developed as **K**—What I Know, **W**—What I Want to Find Out, **L**—What I Learned and Still Need to Learn (Ogle, 1986). The addition of Plus (Carr & Ogle, 1987) adds a writing opportunity for students to summarize their knowledge, add their personal response, and/or organize their learning through the use of a Concept Map or Semantic Map (see reproducible masters on pages 32–34 and 89).

The K-W-L Plus strategy is easy to use and helps students access their knowledge about a topic prior to reading or learning more about it. By developing a list of questions of what students want or expect to learn, they establish purposes for reading and/or learning. The strategy invites students to clarify their preconceptions about the topic by cross-checking after the reading or learning experience. This strategy provides opportunities for misconceptions to be clarified and also may establish the need to obtain additional information in order to answer questions that may not have been addressed in the lesson. The final aspect of the strategy involves having students create a map of information, write a summary of the information learned, and/or write their reactions to the information acquired.

Procedure

1. Make an overhead transparency using the reproducible master on page 80.
2. Select a topic and invite students to think about what they already know about it. Remind them that making connections now will help them better understand the lesson.
3. Write students' ideas under the **K** heading on the transparency.

4. Ask students what they want to know or expect to learn about the topic. Record their questions under the **W** heading on the transparency. You may wish to guide students in thinking about questions that lead toward major concepts in the lesson.

5. Tell students to read the selection, watch the video, listen to the audiotape, or participate in the experiment or field trip, depending on the situation.

6. After the learning experience, have students recall information that they learned. Record their responses under the **L** heading on the transparency. You may also list ideas that they still need to learn here or create another column labeled S (still need to learn).

7. Help students discern or identify broad categories for the ideas under the **L** heading. List these on the transparency or board.

8. Create a Concept Map (see page 32) on the board or on a blank transparency with the topic in the center and the categories of information around it. Ask students to assist in listing each idea from the L section under the appropriate category.

9. Using the Concept Map as a guide, have students work individually or in pairs to create a summary paragraph for each category.

10. As students become proficient with the strategy, provide copies of the K-W-L Plus reproducible master on page 80 to students. Encourage students to use K-W-L Plus in future lessons. Additional reproducible masters with variations of this strategy are found on pages 81–82.

References

Carr, E., & Ogle, D. (1987). K-W-L Plus: A strategy for comprehension and summarization. *Journal of Reading, 30,* 626–631.

Ogle, D. M. (1986). K-W-L: A teaching model that develops active reading of expository text. *The Reading Teacher, 39,* 564–570.

Sample K-W-L Plus
for Intermediate Grade Science

K-W-L Plus Strategy Sheet

Insect-Eating Plants

K	W	L
WHAT WE KNOW	**WHAT WE WANT TO FIND OUT**	**WHAT WE LEARNED**
Venus flytrap	Why do they eat insects?	N-Plants get nitrogen from insects and spiders.
eat hamburger	How do they get insects to stay?	L-Plants live in swampy areas.
leaves open and close	Are there many plants that eat insects?	P-Plants set traps and wait for insects to come by.
live in wet places	Where are they found?	L-Pitcher plants live in many parts of the United States.
small		P-Digestive fluid dissolves the insects.
eat insects		K-Pitcher plants
		K-Venus flytrap

C

CATEGORIES OF INFORMATION

L = Location
K = Kinds
P = Process of Eating
N = Need/Uses of Insects

Summary: Pitcher plants and Venus flytraps, two kinds of meat-eating plants, live in swampy areas and get needed nutrients by catching and digesting insects and spiders.

⊛ K-W-L Plus Strategy Sheet

✱ DIRECTIONS

Write the topic of the lesson on the line below. Before the lesson, list what you know under the **K** column. Then think about what you want to know or what you expect you will learn. List these ideas under the **W** column. After the lesson, list what you learned under the **L** column. Then think of categories for the information you learned. List these under the **C** section.

_____

K WHAT WE KNOW	W WHAT WE WANT TO FIND OUT	L WHAT WE LEARNED

C

CATEGORIES OF INFORMATION

Summary:

Based on Carr and Ogle (1987) and Ogle (1986). From Jerry L. Johns and Roberta L. Berglund, *Strategies for Content Area Learning* (2nd ed.). Copyright © 2006 by Kendall/Hunt Publishing Company (1-800-247-3458, ext. 4). May be reproduced for noncommercial educational purposes. www.kendallhunt.com/readingresources.html

KEL

(What we *Know;* what we *Expect* to find out; what we *Learned.*)

Name _____ Date _____

Work read _____

K: What we KNOW	
E: What we EXPECT to find out	**L: What we LEARNED**

K-W-L Chart

Name _____ Date _____

What we think we **Know**	Were we correct?	Where we found it	What we **Want** to know	What we **Learned**	Where we found it

List-Group-Label
(Semantic Mapping)

FOCUS	TEXT	WHEN	WHY	HOW
✓Vocabulary	✓Narrative	✓Before Reading	Connecting Questioning	✓Individual
✓Comprehension	✓Informational	During Reading	✓Synthesizing Inferring	✓Small Group
Response		✓After Reading	✓Determining Importance	✓Whole Group

DESCRIPTION

List-Group-Label, also known as Semantic Mapping, when graphically represented (Heimlich & Pittelman, 1986; Johnson & Pearson, 1984; Pearson & Johnson, 1978; Taba, 1967), helps students to organize information in categorical form. By classifying and categorizing information, students become active readers and, in the process, remember new vocabulary and information.

Procedure

1. Choose a major concept or topic being studied by the class. In high school health class, for example, the topic of drug use is a key area.

2. List words related to the topic on the board or overhead transparency. Ask students to brainstorm words related to the topic. For example, words related to drug use might be *medicine, illness, substance abuse, illegal drugs, synthetic drugs, gateway drugs, overdose, withdrawal, side effects, addiction, dependence,* and *tolerance.* Try to keep the number of responses to twenty or twenty-five for ease of management.

3. When the brainstormed words have been listed, read them aloud and ask students to cluster the words into smaller groups based on shared relationships. This can be done in list form (List-Group-Label reproducible on page 86) or in graphic form (Semantic Map reproducible on page 89). Students need to label clusters or give them titles to indicate what the words have in common. You may wish to have students complete this step in small cooperative groups. It is often possible for some of the brainstormed words to become category headings. For example, the labels for clusters related to drug use might be: *Helpful Uses of Drugs, Harmful Uses of Drugs,* and *Dangers of Substance Abuse.*

4. When students have completed their classification and categorization of the words, invite students to share the labels for each of their clusters and the words they have included under each heading. You may wish to record these on the board or on an overhead transparency created from the reproducible master on page 86.

5. It is important that students share their reasons for their clustering decisions. This sharing stimulates students to think of the words in a variety of ways, consider their meanings, connect them, and see relationships among the words.

6. If used as a prereading activity, ask students to read the text and evaluate their classifications. They may need to rearrange some words based on additional information in the lesson.

7. If used as a postreading activity, students may want to return to the text and confirm their reasons for and accuracy of their clusters. Students may also wish to use their completed lists or semantic maps as a study aid.

8. The strategy work can be extended over the course of several days as students acquire additional information about the topic. More words can be added to the clusters as students expand their knowledge and increase the connections they make between and among the words. If desired, different colored inks can be used for words added from additional sources or at different times, thus graphically illustrating the expanding knowledge base of the students and the desirability of using a variety of resources in acquiring information.

9. When the lists or semantic maps are complete, have students work individually or in pairs to write a summary of the information in one of the clusters or write a longer piece about the topic, using each one of the clusters of information as a paragraph in the longer piece.

References

Heimlich, J. E., & Pittelman, S. D. (1986). *Semantic mapping: Classroom applications.* Newark, DE: International Reading Association.

Johnson, D. D., & Pearson, P. D. (1984). *Teaching reading vocabulary* (2nd ed.). New York: Holt, Rinehart & Winston.

Pearson, P. D., & Johnson, D. D. (1978). *Teaching reading comprehension.* New York: Holt, Rinehart & Winston.

Taba, H. (1967). *Teacher's handbook for elementary social studies.* Reading, MA: Addison-Wesley.

Sample List-Group-Label Developed from a High School Health Lesson on the **Nervous System**

<u>Nervous System</u>
(topic)

1. Brainstorm a list of words related to the topic given to you by your teacher. Write the topic on the line above and list the words that are related to it in the space below.

brain	brain stem	autonomic
somatic	sympathetic	reflexes
cerebellum	spinal cord	parasympathetic
cerebrum	meninges	nerves

2. Now consider how some of the words listed above might be related. Think of ways they might be grouped together by their meanings. Write the title of the categories or headings on each line below. (You may have a greater or lesser number of words and groupings than the number of lines below.) Then list the words under the appropriate headings. Use the back of this paper for additional words and clusters if you need it.

<u>Central Nervous System</u>
(cluster heading)

1. brain
2. spinal cord
3. cerebellum
4. cerebrum
5. brain stem
6. meninges

<u>Peripheral Nervous System</u>
(cluster heading)

1. autonomic
2. somatic
3. sympathetic
4. parasympathetic
5. reflexes
6. nerves

_____
(cluster heading)

1. _____
2. _____
3. _____
4. _____
5. _____

_____
(cluster heading)

1. _____
2. _____
3. _____
4. _____
5. _____

⊛ List-Group-Label

_____
(topic)

1. Brainstorm a list of words related to the topic given to you by your teacher. Write the topic on the line above and list the words that are related to it in the space below.

2. Now consider how some of the words listed above might be related. Think of ways they might be grouped together by their meanings. Write the title of the categories or headings on each line below. (You may have a greater or lesser number of words and groupings than the number of lines below.) Then list the words under the appropriate headings. Use the back of this paper for additional words and clusters if you need it.

_____
(cluster heading)

1. _____
2. _____
3. _____
4. _____
5. _____

_____
(cluster heading)

1. _____
2. _____
3. _____
4. _____
5. _____

_____
(cluster heading)

1. _____
2. _____
3. _____
4. _____
5. _____

_____
(cluster heading)

1. _____
2. _____
3. _____
4. _____
5. _____

Based on Heimlich and Pittelman (1986), Johnson and Pearson (1984), Pearson and Johnson (1978), and Taba (1967). From Jerry L. Johns and Roberta L. Berglund, _Strategies for Content Area Learning_ (2nd ed.). Copyright © 2006 by Kendall/Hunt Publishing Company (1-800-247-3458, ext. 4). May be reproduced for noncommercial educational purposes. www.kendallhunt.com/readingresources.html

Sample Semantic Map Developed from a High School Health Lesson on the **Nervous System**

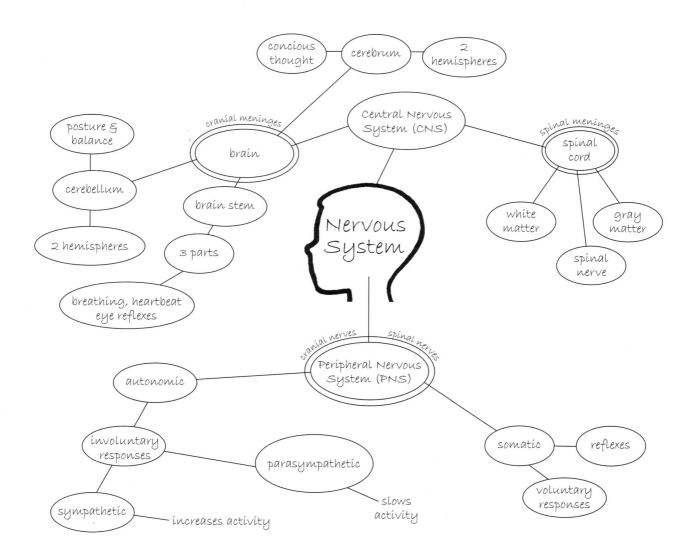

Summary: The brain is one part of the central nervous system. Surrounded by cranial meninges, the brain has three parts: the cerebellum, the cerebrum, and the brain stem. The cerebellum has two hemispheres and controls posture and balance. The cerebrum has two hemispheres and controls conscious thought. The brain stem has three parts and controls breathing, heartbeat, and eye reflexes.

Sample Semantic Map Created after a Lesson on **Insect-Eating Plants**

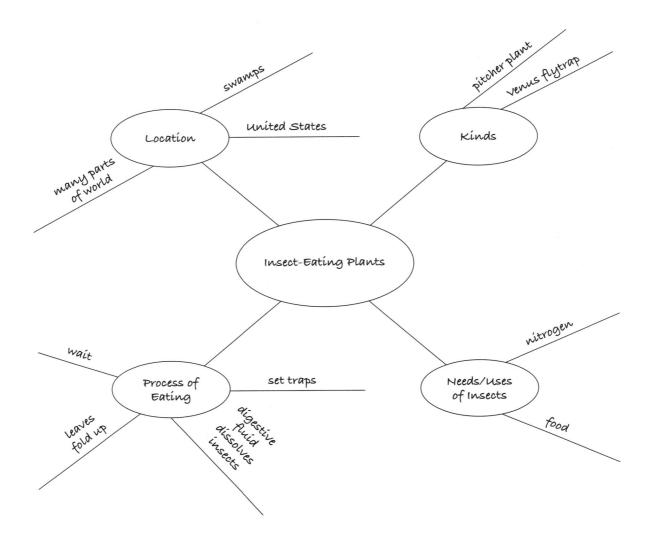

Summary of What We Learned

There are many kinds of insect-eating plants. The Venus flytrap and pitcher plant are two of them.

Insect-eating plants live in swampy areas in many parts of the world. Pitcher plants live in the United States.

Insect-eating plants set traps and wait for unsuspecting insects to come along. Then they capture them and slowly dissolve them using the plants' digestive fluid.

Insect-eating plants get nitrogen from the insects and spiders they eat. That's how they stay alive.

Name _____ Date _____

⊙ Semantic Map

_____
(topic)

☀ DIRECTIONS

Think of ways the ideas from your lesson might be clustered together. Below is one way you might begin to cluster them into categories. You may add to the map below or create a map of your own on the back of this page.

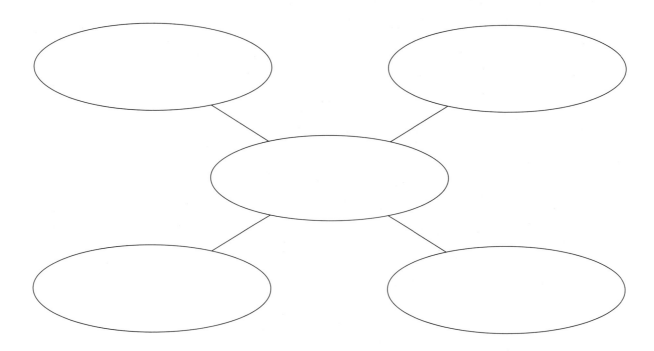

Summary:

People Search

FOCUS	TEXT	WHEN	WHY	HOW
✓Vocabulary	✓Narrative	✓Before Reading	✓Connecting Questioning	Individual
✓Comprehension	✓Informational	During Reading	Synthesizing ✓Inferring	Small Group
✓Response		✓After Reading	Determining Importance	✓Whole Group

DESCRIPTION

People Search (Hemmrich, Lim, & Neel, 1994) invites students to ask other students in the class for information about a topic or area of study. As students seek specific information, they can become more motivated to learn about a topic and may become more engaged in learning. People Search can be used as a way to introduce a new topic or as a review for a unit of study that has been completed.

Procedure

1. Decide which variation of People Search to use: an introduction to a new course or unit of study, a chapter from a text, or as a review technique for concepts, ideas, and details that were taught.

2. Prepare a list of statements relating to the topic or area of study using one of the People Search reproducibles on pages 94–96. For example, if students are going to read *To Kill a Mockingbird,* you might use statements like the following.

   Find someone who has attended a court trial.

   Find someone who has lived in the South.

3. Duplicate the statements in the People Search and give a copy to each student. Explain that they are to circulate in the room and locate classmates who can fit the statement or answer the question. When a classmate is found, he or she should initial or sign on the line beside the item.

   Find someone who has attended a court trial. _____Rosie_____

   Find someone who has lived in the South. _____Chad_____

4. Specify if you want students to have as many different signatures as possible or if there is a limit to the number of times an individual student can sign or initial statements.

5. Provide time for students to circulate among classmates in order to complete the People Search. Expect some noise and spirited interactions. Tell students when they have two minutes left for their search.

6. Have students return to their seats. Engage them in a discussion of their search. The discussion can be in small groups or with the entire class. Invite students who signed statements to share with the entire class. For example, if Rosie attended a court trial, have her share a bit about the experience. If both Patrice and Chad lived in the South, have them share where they lived and what it was like. They could also compare it to where they now live.

Sample People Search for Art (Advanced Drawing Terminology Review)

✳ DIRECTIONS

Find another student who can name the term that matches each definition. Ask him or her to initial the corresponding square IF you agree with the answer. If you think he or she is wrong, move on to another student. Each person can initial no more than three squares. [Note: The answers are in capital letters.]

lightness or darkness VALUE	combining elements by using step by step changes GRADATION	combining elements to add stability to the artwork BALANCE
combining elements into complicated relationships VARIETY	how the elements in an artwork are organized using the principles COMPOSITION	the relationship of elements/parts to the whole PROPORTION
combining similar elements throughout an artwork HARMONY	another name for color HUE	the way something feels TEXTURE
drawing objects to look three-dimensional PERSPECTIVE	brightness or dullness INTENSITY	things far away are lighter, less colorful, fewer details AERIAL PERSPECTIVE

Reference

Hemmrich, H., Lim, W., & Neel, K. (1994). *Primetime!* Portsmouth, NH: Heinemann.

Sample People Search
for **Literature**

✳ **DIRECTIONS**

Before we begin reading *To Kill a Mockingbird,* find other students who can relate to the sentences. Have the student sign his or her name. No student can be listed more than twice. You have seven minutes to try to complete your search.

1. Find someone who vividly remembers his or her first day of school. _____

2. Find someone who has been scared of a neighbor in the past. _____

3. Find someone who secretly gave a nice gift to someone else. _____

4. Find someone who has had a fire in his or her home. _____

5. Find someone who has attended a court trial. _____

6. Find someone who has a friend he or she sees every summer, only in the summer. _____

7. Find someone who knows someone who has run away. _____

8. Find someone who has experienced prejudice. _____

9. Find someone who has lived in the South. _____

Thanks are extended to Angie Currier, Indianapolis, IN for sharing this idea. From Jerry L. Johns and Roberta L. Berglund, *Strategies for Content Area Learning* (2nd ed.). Copyright © 2006 by Kendall/Hunt Publishing Company (1-800-247-3458, ext. 4). May be reproduced for noncommercial educational purposes. www.kendallhunt.com/readingresources.html

Name _____ Date _____

⊛ People Search

☀ DIRECTIONS

Find other students who "fit" the statement or can answer the question. The same student can sign two of the items.

Statement/Questions	Student
1. _____	_____
_____	
2. _____	_____
_____	
3. _____	_____
_____	
4. _____	_____
_____	
5. _____	_____
_____	
6. _____	_____
_____	
7. _____	_____
_____	
8. _____	_____
_____	
9. _____	_____
_____	
10. _____	_____
_____	

★ People Search

✳ DIRECTIONS

Find another student _____

_____

_____

_____

People Search Bingo

✳ DIRECTIONS

Read the items in the boxes. Select one or two that apply to you. Write your name in no more than two boxes. Now find classmates who can sign their names in the other boxes, no more than two per person. When you fill a row, column or diagonal with signatures, you win People Search Bingo!

		FREE		

Plot/Concept Relationships

FOCUS	TEXT	WHEN	WHY	HOW
Vocabulary	✓Narrative	Before Reading	✓Connecting Questioning	✓Individual
✓Comprehension	✓Informational	During Reading	✓Synthesizing ✓Inferring	Small Group
✓Response		✓After Reading	✓Determining Importance	Whole Group

DESCRIPTION

Originally called the Plot Relationships chart (Schmidt & Buckley, 1991), this strategy can be used with narrative text to teach story grammar and with informational text to teach students cause-effect relationships. When students complete the Plot/Concept Relationships chart, they are visually representing the connections between characters in stories, events in history, hierarchical concepts in science, or steps of inquiry in science.

Procedure

1. To teach plot relationships, choose a story that has clear elements of plot such as characters, goal, problem, and solution. To teach cause-effect relationships, choose an informational text that has clear examples of events that lead to other events, for example, the events leading to Haiti's independence from France. To teach scientific concepts or steps of inquiry, choose a science text that has clear conceptual definitions or that states procedural steps of inquiry.

2. Use an example you develop or the sample Plot Relationships chart on page 99 to model for students how to use the strategy.

3. Make an overhead transparency and duplicate copies of the Plot Relationships reproducible master on page 101 or adapt it to suit your needs or purposes.

4. To model plot relationships, review with students the basic elements of a story; that is, stories usually have main characters, a goal the characters wish to achieve, problems that prevent them from achieving the goal, and a solution to the problem. In the sample Plot Relationships chart, a story from a middle school reading text is used.

5. Read through the four boxes in the sample with students. Ask them to generate full sentences using the information in all four boxes. For example, "Carlos wanted to buy a new camera lens, but he did not have enough money, so he had to work more hours to earn the money."

6. Instruct students to read the story you chose for them and to use the strategy to first complete the four boxes. Then have students write out the complete sentence containing the basic information.

7. To model concept relationships, review with students how to determine cause and effect by looking for key words such as *because, when,* and *if-then.* In the two sample Concept Relationships charts on page 100, passages from a middle school social studies text and a middle school science text are used.

8. Read through the four boxes in the sample with students and then ask them to generate full sentences using the information in all four boxes. For example, in the science sample, "Because humans are warm-blooded and breathe by lungs and sharks are cold-blooded and breathe by gills, humans are different from sharks."

9. Move on to the informational text you chose for the students. Instruct students to use the strategy to first complete the four boxes and then write out the complete sentence.

10. Demonstrate another type of Concept Relationships chart with headings of "Problem," "Hypothesis," "Testing," and "Conclusion." This sample chart is shown on page 100. Discuss with students when this chart would be more appropriate for use than the other type of chart. For example, when a question is posed in science, this second chart is more appropriate. When a cause and effect relationship is delineated, the first chart is more appropriate.

11. Encourage students to use a Plot/Concept Relationships chart whenever they need to demonstrate comprehension of text.

Reference

Schmidt, B., & Buckley, M. (1991). Plot relationships chart. In J. M. Macon, D. Bewell, & M. Vogt (Eds.), *Responses to literature: Grades K–8* (pp. 7–8). Newark, DE: International Reading Association.

Sample Plot Relationships
for Middle School **Literature**

SOMEBODY	WANTED	BUT	SO
Carlos	to buy a new camera lens	he didn't have enough money	he had to work more hours to earn the money.

Carlos wanted to buy a new camera lens, but he didn't have enough money, so he had to work more hours to earn the money.

Sample Concept Relationships
for Middle School **Science**

SOMEBODY	WANTED	BUT	SO
The Australian Aborigines	to raise wild dogs called dingoes	the dingoes did not belong there and ate too many other animals	other animals like the Tasmanian devil became extinct on mainland Australia.

The Australian Aborigines wanted to raise wild dogs called dingoes. But the dingoes did not belong there in Australia, and they ate too many of the other animals. Because the dingoes ate so many of the Tasmanian devils, now the Tasmanian devils are extinct on the mainland of Australia.

Sample Concept Relationships
for Middle School **Social Studies**

SOMEBODY	WANTED	BUT	SO
Haiti	freedom from France	had to defeat Napoleon's troops	the Haitian rebel army kept fighting until they won their independence.

Haiti wanted freedom from France, but Napoleon and his troops were in control, so the Haitian rebel army kept fighting until they won their independence.

Sample Concept Relationships
for Middle School **Science**

PROBLEM	HYPOTHESIS	TESTING	CONCLUSION
What makes humans different from sharks?	Humans are mammals, sharks are fish.	Mammals are warm-blooded and breathe by lungs. Fish are cold-blooded and breathe by gills.	Humans are warm-blooded and breathe by lungs, and sharks are cold-blooded and breathe by gills. Therefore, humans are different from sharks.

Because humans are warm-blooded and breathe by lungs and sharks are cold-blooded and breathe by gills, humans are different from sharks.

Name _____ Date _____

 Plot/Concept Relationships

SOMEBODY	WANTED	BUT	SO

_____

_____

_____

_____

_____

_____

_____

Name _____ Date _____

◉ Concept Relationships

PROBLEM	HYPOTHESIS	TESTING	CONCLUSION

_____

_____

_____

_____

_____

_____

_____

Possible Sentences

FOCUS	TEXT	WHEN	WHY	HOW
✓Vocabulary	✓Narrative	✓Before Reading	✓Connecting Questioning	✓Individual
Comprehension	✓Informational	During Reading	Synthesizing ✓Inferring	✓Small Group
✓Response		✓After Reading	Determining Importance	✓Whole Group

DESCRIPTION

The Possible Sentences strategy (Moore & Moore, 1992; Readence, Bean, & Baldwin, 2004) is used to help students predict the content in a selection and then check their predictions while reading. After reading, students use the text to support the accuracy of their predictions or revise them so they are more reflective of the content. The Possible Sentences strategy helps students set a purpose for reading and develop interest in and curiosity about the text. Through the use of the strategy, students formulate questions that they wish to answer by reading, make connections to their background knowledge, and, based on the vocabulary selected, make inferences about the content of the text.

Procedure

1. List 10–15 key vocabulary words (some new, some familiar) from a text selection on the board, overhead transparency, or reproducible master (page 105) and pronounce the words for the students.

2. Ask students to select at least two words from the list and use them in a sentence that they believe might reflect the content of the passage. Stress that students are using their prior knowledge about the words. Perhaps these words remind them of something they know about. Encourage them to write their sentences in the space provided on the reproducible master.

3. Ask students to share their sentences orally. Write them on the board or overhead transparency as they are given, underlining words from the list. Continue until all the words have been used or until the available time has elapsed.

4. Have students read the text selection.

5. After reading, have students reread each sentence and determine its accuracy. Rate it **T** (true), **F** (false), or **DK** (don't know—not enough information given). Revise or omit those sentences that are not accurate and those about which insufficient information was provided in the text. Encourage students to cite specific text references in making their conclusions about sentence accuracy. After the sentences are corrected or verified to be correct, students could be asked to enter them into their notebooks or class log books.

Sample Possible Sentences for Middle School **Social Studies**

<u>_____Ancient Rome_____</u>
(topic)

Below are some words that you will find in your reading.

republic	dictator	veto	forum	aqueduct
persecute	martyr	legion	disciple	census

Possible Sentences

✳ DIRECTIONS

Write one or more sentences using at least two of the above terms in each sentence. Underline the words from the list above. After reading, rate the accuracy of each sentence by indicating True (T), False (F), or Don't Know (DK).

___F___ 1. One citizen became a <u>martyr</u> when he sacrificed his life rather than carry out the commands of the <u>dictator</u>.

___T___ 2. The members of the <u>forum</u> conducted a <u>census</u> of the population to determine the ages and locations of everyone in the <u>republic</u>.

___DK___ 3. Some of the members of the <u>legion</u> supported the building of an <u>aqueduct</u> to bring needed water to the town.

Key
T = True
F = False, needs to be rewritten
DK = Don't know, information not given in the reading

References

Moore, D. W., & Moore, S. A. (1992). Possible sentences: An update. In E. K. Dishner, T. W. Bean, J. E. Readence, & D. W. Moore (Eds.), *Reading in the content areas: Improving classroom instruction* (3rd ed.) (pp. 196–202). Dubuque, IA: Kendall/Hunt.

Readence, J. E., Bean, T. W., & Baldwin, R. S. (2004). *Content area literacy: An integrated approach* (8th ed.). Dubuque, IA: Kendall/Hunt.

Name _____ Date _____

 # Possible Sentences

_____
(topic)

Below are some words that you will find in your reading.

_____	_____	_____
_____	_____	_____
_____	_____	_____
_____	_____	_____
_____	_____	_____

Possible Sentences

✳ DIRECTIONS

Write one or more sentences using at least two of the above terms in each sentence. Underline the words from the list above. After reading, rate the accuracy of each sentence by indicating True (T), False (F), or Don't Know (DK).

_____ 1. _____

_____

_____ 2. _____

_____

_____ 3. _____

_____

_____ 4. _____

_____

_____ 5. _____

_____

Key
T = True
F = False, needs to be rewritten
DK = Don't know, information not given in the reading

Based on Moore and Moore (1992). From Jerry L. Johns and Roberta L. Berglund, *Strategies for Content Area Learning* (2nd ed.). Copyright © 2006 by Kendall/Hunt Publishing Company (1-800-247-3458, ext. 4). May be reproduced for noncommercial educational purposes. www.kendallhunt.com/readingresources.html

Question-Answer Relationships (QARs)

FOCUS	TEXT	WHEN	WHY	HOW
Vocabulary	✓Narrative	Before Reading	✓Connecting ✓Questioning	✓Individual
✓Comprehension	✓Informational	During Reading	✓Synthesizing ✓Inferring	Small Group
Response		✓After Reading	✓Determining Importance	Whole Group

DESCRIPTION

Question-Answer Relationships (Raphael, 1982, 1986) help students to determine where and how to find answers to questions. There are two main categories of questions: *in the book QARs* and *in my head QARs*. The two "in the book" questions, "right there" and "putting it together" have answers supplied by the author. The two "in my head" questions, "author and me" and "on-my-own," have answers either partially or entirely based on students' knowledge and experiences (Buehl, 2001). Raphael and Pearson (1982) found that students in grades four, six, and eight who were taught the QAR strategy were more successful at answering questions than those students who were not taught the strategy. QARs are valuable for helping students to make the transition from explicitly stated information in texts to the often implicitly stated information found in more advanced reading materials.

Procedure

1. Ask students how they find information when they are asked to answer comprehension questions after reading an assignment. Discuss the various ways they cope with the challenge of answering difficult questions. Also, highlight just what it is that makes the questions difficult. For example, are they difficult because the information is not readily available? Or are they difficult because students must formulate their own conclusions? Use this discussion to introduce QARs.

2. Make an overhead transparency and duplicate copies of the Question-Answer Relationships (QARs) reproducible master on page 110 or adapt it to suit your needs or purposes. Show the students the QARs overhead transparency. Explain to students that as they progress through school, the types of questions they will be expected to answer become more challenging partly because the answers can come from a variety of places. You may also want to make an overhead transparency of the reproducible on page 111 to help introduce the types of QARs.

3. Read aloud to students the sample passage on page 109 or white out the answers and distribute a sheet to each student. You could also use an example from your curriculum. Then model for students how you decide where to find the answers. If the questions are explicitly from the text, they are "right there" questions. Invite a student to show in the passage where the answer can be found. If the questions can be answered by using information from several places in the text, they are "putting it together" questions. Invite a student to show where connections in the passage can be made. If the questions involve looking for clues the author may have given, they are "author and me" questions. Invite a student to point out clues the author has given in the passage. And finally, if the questions require students to use their own knowledge and experiences, they are "on my own" questions. Model for students how to base answers on their own experiences and knowledge. Students may not agree with all the answers on page 109. You may also want to use the large visuals found on the CD-ROM for the four types of QARs.

4. Prepare a short text passage that contains information that you can use to create the four types of QAR questions. Include one or two of each type of question on the page. Either reproduce this passage for students or put it on an overhead transparency. You will use this passage when the students are ready to try the strategy on their own.

5. Distribute or display the passage and prepare some questions to practice QARs. Instruct students to first read the passage silently, then identify the nature of each question asked after the passage. You may also wish to have students actually answer the questions. Take time to allow students to share their opinions about the types of questions asked and discuss how they decided the types of questions.

6. Distribute copies of the QAR reproducible. Instruct students to refer to the sheet whenever they are asked to answer questions after reading and ask them to put the initials of the question type by each of their written answers. For example, if the question is "right-there," students will write *RT* next to their answer. A suggested key is below.

   RT = Right There
   PT = Putting It Together
   AAM = Author and Me
   OMO = On-My-Own

7. In subsequent lessons, help students understand that QARs can help them know where they will get information to answer questions in their reading.

Additional reproducibles can be found on the CD-ROM accompanying this book.

References

Buehl, D. (2001). *Classroom strategies for interactive learning* (2nd ed.). Newark, DE: International Reading Association.

Raphael, T. E. (1982). Question-answering strategies for children. *The Reading Teacher, 36,* 186–190.

Raphael, T. E. (1986). Teaching Question-Answer Relationships, revisited. *The Reading Teacher, 39,* 516–522.

Raphael, T. E., & Pearson, P. D. (1982). *The effect of metacognitive training on children's question-answering behavior.* Urbana, IL: Center for the Study of Reading.

Sample Question-Answer Relationships for Middle School Science

The Life Sciences

Careers in life sciences can be divided into two major groups: the biology professions and the health professions. The professions in biology include many kinds of specialists who are involved in research and teaching. In general, entrance into these careers requires many years of college training plus original research.

Most biologists who study animals specialize in one group. For example, scientists called ichthyologists study fish, entomologists study insects, and herpetologists study reptiles and amphibians. Anatomists and physiologists study the structure of living organisms and the functioning of their bodies. Cytologists are biologists who study cells.

1. What do most biologists do in addition to teaching? (Answer: PIT)

Right There

Putting It Together

Author and Me

On My Own

2. What are the two major groups of careers in life sciences? (Answer: RT)

Right There

Putting It Together

Author and Me

On My Own

3. How many years must one go to college to be a biologist? (Answer: OMO)

Right There

Putting It Together

Author and Me

On My Own

4. What is the suffix, or word ending, used to describe careers in biology? (Answer: AAM)

Right There

Putting It Together

Author and Me

On My Own

Name _____ Date _____

  # Question-Answer Relationships (QARs)

 **Right There**

 Putting It Together

Author and Me

 On My Own

In-The-Book Questions

 Right There: The answer to the question is right in the book. You can look for key words to help you find the answer.

 **Putting It Together:** The answer is in the book, but not as easy to find. You may have to combine pieces of information from different places in the book.

In-My-Head Questions

 Author and Me: The author may have given hints or clues that you combine with what you know to help you to figure out the answer.

 **On My Own:** The answer is in your head. These are the questions that you really have to take time to think through. You may have to think about what you already know or about experiences you've had.

Based on Raphael (1982, 1986). From Jerry L. Johns and Roberta L. Berglund, *Strategies for Content Area Learning* (2nd ed.). Copyright © 2006 by Kendall/Hunt Publishing Company (1-800-247-3458, ext. 4). May be reproduced for noncommercial educational purposes. www.kendallhunt.com/readingresources.html

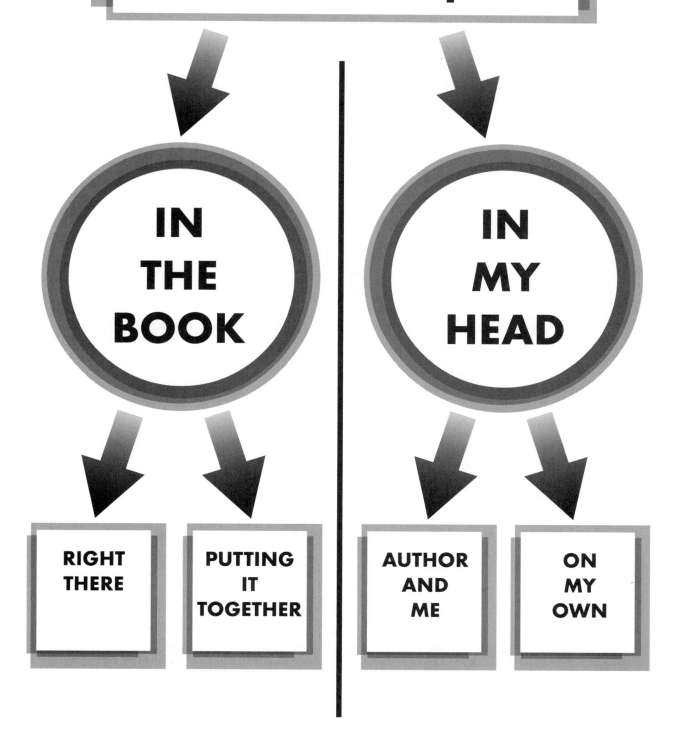

Role, Audience,
Format, Topic (RAFT)

FOCUS	TEXT	WHEN	WHY	HOW
Vocabulary	✓Narrative	Before Reading	Connecting Questioning	✓Individual
Comprehension	✓Informational	During Reading	✓Synthesizing ✓Inferring	Small Group
✓Response		✓After Reading	✓Determining Importance	Whole Group

DESCRIPTION

RAFT (Role, Audience, Format, Topic) (Santa, Havens, & Valdes, 2004) is a strategy that is useful in all content areas. It encourages students to write from a viewpoint other than their own and in a form that may be more unusual than common. The purpose is to provide opportunities for students to demonstrate their understanding of a topic or subject through a writing experience that helps them to think about the subject and communicate their understanding of it in a creative and sometimes entertaining and interesting way. RAFT writing assignments often motivate students to write in an in-depth and organized fashion and, in the process, help them to think about and more fully understand the subject being studied.

Procedure

1. Consider the major concepts of the chapter, unit, or selection being used in your classroom.
2. Consider possible roles that students might assume. For example, if the class is studying Ancient Rome, possible roles might be a gladiator's sword, a member of the tribunal or senate, a Roman general, a chariot, or a Roman coin.
3. Decide on possible audiences, formats, and topics for the assignment that might help students extend their understanding of what the class is studying. For example, if Ancient Rome is the topic, audiences might be slave owners, mercenary soldiers, tourists, or citizens of Rome. Formats might be a newspaper editorial, a journal entry, a speech, an advertisement, a travel brochure, or a eulogy. Possible topics might include discouraging violence in Rome, proposing cooperation with another government, justifying service in the Roman army, conducting a guided tour of Ancient Rome, or possibly mourning the death of the Roman empire.

4. Prepare a RAFT assignment for your students listing the possible roles, audiences, formats, and topics they might use.

5. Present the concept of RAFT to your students, including its four components, and share some examples with them. (See the RAFT examples on pages 115 and 116).

6. Have students choose their roles and then work in small groups with students who have selected the same role to brainstorm possible information and emotions that might be shared through the role of the writer.

7. Finally, have students select their audience, format, and topic and begin work.

8. Because RAFT assignments vary a great deal, it is helpful to share a rubric for grading the work at the outset so that students understand the criteria on which they will be judged. Areas of the rubric might include: writing was appropriate for intended audience; writing followed chosen format; information presented was accurate; grammar and mechanics were acceptable. Selected areas can be weighted for greater emphasis. Be sure to star (*) these areas on the reproducible master before reproducing it.

9. As students gain greater competence with RAFT, they can help determine what to use for the four RAFT elements (Role, Audience, Format, Topic).

Reference

Santa, C. M., Havens, L. T., & Valdes, B. J. (2004). *Project CRISS: Creating independence through student-owned strategies* (3rd ed.). Dubuque, IA: Kendall/Hunt.

Sample RAFT Assignment
for Intermediate Grade Students
Studying the **Revolutionary War**

✳ DIRECTIONS

Consider the RAFT possibilities listed below. Choose your role and circle it. Now discuss that role with others who have selected the same one. Consider the following in your discussion.

1. Describe me.
2. What feelings do I have?
3. What information do I need to convey through my writing?
4. What words or ideas might I include to get my point across?
5. What do I know about my audience? What type of information or persuasion might they need?
6. What do I already know about the format? How might it look?

ROLE	AUDIENCE	FORMAT	TOPIC
Young Colonist Boy	Sons of Liberty	Resume	Wants to Join
Paul Revere's Horse	Other War Horses	Memo	The Midnight Ride
Patriot Soldier	Your Family	Letter Home	Reality of War
Colonist	King	Speech	Stop Unfair Taxation
Tea	Colonists	Editorial	Stop Boston Tea Party
News Reporter	Future Generations	News Release	Tell Why Boston Massacre Was Significant
American Flag	British Citizens	Poem	Freedom

When you have finished your discussion, you may begin your work. Your RAFT assignment should be at least one page in length and will be judged using the following criteria. The starred (*) items are worth double points.

Completed on Time	1	2	3	4	5
Writing Appropriate for Audience*	1	2	3	4	5
Format Followed	1	2	3	4	5
Information Accurate*	1	2	3	4	5
Grammar and Mechanics	1	2	3	4	5
Neatness	1	2	3	4	5
Creativity	1	2	3	4	5

Sample RAFT Assignment for Middle School Students Studying **Ancient Greece**

✱ DIRECTIONS

Consider the RAFT possibilities listed below. Choose your role and circle it. Now discuss that role with others who have selected the same one. Consider the following in your discussion.

1. Describe me.
2. What feelings do I have?
3. What information do I need to convey through my writing?
4. What words or ideas might I include to get my point across?
5. What do I know about my audience? What type of information or persuasion might they need?
6. What do I already know about the format? How might it look?

ROLE	AUDIENCE	FORMAT	TOPIC
Socrates	The Athenian Court	Plea	Spare His Life
Alexander's Sword	Self	Diary	Living with Alexander the Great
Corinthian Column	Greek Architects	Resume	Job Application
Hermes	Zeus	Letter	Work Overload
Letter F	Greek Alphabet	Memo	Wishes to Join the Greek Alphabet
Grapes and Olives	Tourists	Travel Brochure	Visit Greece
Ship	Greek Traders	Advertisement	Hire Me

When you have finished your discussion, you may begin your work. Your RAFT assignment should be at least one page in length and will be judged using the following criteria. The starred (*) items are worth double points.

Completed on Time*	1	2	3	4	5
Writing Appropriate for Audience	1	2	3	4	5
Format Followed*	1	2	3	4	5
Information Accurate*	1	2	3	4	5
Grammar and Mechanics	1	2	3	4	5
Neatness	1	2	3	4	5
Creativity	1	2	3	4	5

Sample RAFT Assignments

ROLE	AUDIENCE	FORMAT	TOPIC
Sue, the T-Rex Dinosaur	Paleontologist	Memoir	Life in the Time of Dinosaurs
Newspaper Columnist	Jury	Testimonial	Freedom of Speech
Flight Attendant	Pilots	Proposal	Equal Pay
Chef	Cooking Class	Instructions	How to Create the Perfect Meal
Semicolon	High School Students	Complaint Letter	How It Is Misused
Meteorologist	Hurricanes	Statistics	How They Compare
Student Body President	Principal	Proposal	Reasons Why Longer Lunch Hour Needed
Naturalist John Muir	Lumber Industry	Commercial	Conservation of Natural Resources
Michelangelo	Pope	Bill	Services Provided during Painting of Sistine Chapel
Salmon	Grand Coulee Dam	Flyer	Difficulties Caused by Dam
Fraction	Whole Number	Letter	How They Are Different How They Should Work Together
Soil	Earthworm	Menu	Soil Varieties
Blood	Doctor	Travelogue	Movement through Body
Triangle	Mathematician	Appeal	Why It Is Needed
Muscles	Treadmill	Love Letter	Benefits of Exercise
Plant	Water	Thank You Note	Benefits of Water
Harry Potter	Children	Poem	The Wonders of Wizardry
Basketball	New Player	Advice Column	Tips for Success
Auctioneer	Customers	List	Paintings for Sale
Self	Book Character	Yearbook Inscription	Best Character Traits

Sample RAFT
Assignments

ROLE	AUDIENCE	FORMAT	TOPIC
Book Character	Another character in the book	Letter	Ask for suggestions for solving the problem in the story
Main Character	Students	Advice Column	Ask for help solving the conflict in the story
Animal in Rainforest	General Public	Letter to the Editor	Saving the Rainforest
Big Foot	General Public	Letter/News Story	Why I really exist
Cell Organelle	Boss/Employee	Resume	What I can do for the cell
MRNA	Parents/Friends	Letter from Camp	Describe protein synthesis
Teacher	Incoming Students	Letter	Advice
Greek God	Other Gods	Letter	Opinions on what is happening from the poem
Reporter	Public—Choose either a Northern or Southern Perspective	Newspaper	Events leading up to the Civil War (i.e., Bleeding Kansas, John Brown)
Sec/csc/cot	Calculator Company	Letter	Reasons to get own button on calculator
Pencil	Math Teacher	Recipe	Steps to solve a word problem
Teacher	Little Brother, Sister, or Parent	Lesson (conversation and dialogues)	Teach the concept of inertia

From Jerry L. Johns and Roberta L. Berglund, *Strategies for Content Area Learning* (2nd ed.). Copyright © 2006 by Kendall/Hunt Publishing Company (1-800-247-3458, ext. 4). May be reproduced for noncommercial educational purposes. www.kendallhunt.com/readingresources.html

 # RAFT

❊ DIRECTIONS

Consider the RAFT possibilities listed below. Choose your role and circle it. Now discuss that role with others who have selected the same one. Consider the following in your discussion:

1. Describe me.
2. What feelings do I have?
3. What information do I need to convey through my writing?
4. What words or ideas might I include to get my point across?
5. What do I know about my audience? What type of information or persuasion might they need?
6. What do I already know about the format? How might it look?

ROLE	AUDIENCE	FORMAT	TOPIC

When you have finished your discussion, you may begin your work. Your RAFT assignment should be at least one page in length and will be judged using the following criteria. If items are starred (*), they are worth double points.

Completed on Time	1	2	3	4	5
Writing Appropriate for Audience	1	2	3	4	5
Format Followed	1	2	3	4	5
Information Accurate	1	2	3	4	5
Grammar and Mechanics	1	2	3	4	5
Neatness	1	2	3	4	5
Creativity	1	2	3	4	5

Based on Santa, Havens, & Valdes (2004). From Jerry L. Johns and Roberta L. Berglund, *Strategies for Content Area Learning* (2nd ed.). Copyright © 2006 by Kendall/Hunt Publishing Company (1-800-247-3458, ext. 4). May be reproduced for noncommercial educational purposes. www.kendallhunt.com/readingresources.html

Name _____ Date _____

Topic _____ Period _____

RAFT Paper

Role _____ Format _____

Audience _____ Topic _____

_____

_____

_____

_____

_____

_____

_____

_____

_____

_____

_____

_____

_____

_____

_____

_____

_____

_____

Name _____ Date _____

RAFT Rubric

Role _____ Format _____

Audience _____ Topic _____

Completed on Time	1	2	3	4	5
Writing Appropriate for Audience	1	2	3	4	5
Format Followed	1	2	3	4	5
Information Accurate	1	2	3	4	5
Grammar and Mechanics	1	2	3	4	5
Neatness	1	2	3	4	5
Creativity	1	2	3	4	5
_____	1	2	3	4	5
_____	1	2	3	4	5
_____	1	2	3	4	5

Total Points _____

If items are starred (*), they are worth double points.

From Jerry L. Johns and Roberta L. Berglund, *Strategies for Content Area Learning* (2nd ed.). Copyright © 2006 by Kendall/Hunt Publishing Company (1-800-247-3458, ext. 4). May be reproduced for noncommercial educational purposes. www.kendallhunt.com/readingresources.html

Save the Last Word for Me

FOCUS	TEXT	WHEN	WHY	HOW
Vocabulary	✓Narrative	Before Reading	✓Connecting ✓Questioning	✓Individual
Comprehension	✓Informational	✓During Reading	✓Synthesizing ✓Inferring	✓Small Group
✓Response		✓After Reading	Determining Importance	Whole Group

DESCRIPTION

Save the Last Word for Me (Short, Harste, & Burke, 1996; Vaughan & Estes, 1986) is a useful strategy in all content areas. With this strategy, students are encouraged to take an active role in selecting and responding to sections of a text that they find interesting or about which they have a reaction. They then have an opportunity to discuss their choices with other students. One of the advantages of Save the Last Word for Me is that everyone has an opportunity to comment before the student who shares the quote comments about it. This procedure allows the student to consider additional ideas and to add to or delete ideas from his or her original response prior to sharing it with others.

Procedure

1. Distribute three 3×5-inch cards to each student or make copies of the Save the Last Word for Me reproducible master on page 126 and distribute one to each student.

2. Have each student read the selected text independently.

3. As students read, have them lightly mark with pencil sentences or small sections of the text about which they have a reaction, question, or connection.

4. After reading, have students select three of the sentences or sections of text they have marked and write each on an index card or on their copy of the Save the Last Word for Me reproducible.

5. Students then need to write their comments and thoughts about each of the text segments on the back of the cards or on the Save the Last Word for Me reproducible. When this task is completed, place students in groups of 4 or 5 students. You may want to make an overhead transparency of page 127 and use it to highlight the procedures that follow. The Discussion Guide can also be referred to as students share.

6. Choose one student in each group to begin. That student reads one of the text segments he or she has selected. Only the text segment is shared at this time.

7. Each member of the group is then invited to comment on the first student's text segment or quote.

8. When all students in the group have commented, then the student who shared the quote offers his or her comments about it. The comments may or may not be the same as the original thoughts or ideas that were written.

9. The process continues by having another student share a quote from one of the cards or the Save the Last Word for Me reproducible.

10. At the conclusion of the lesson, ask students if selecting the sentences and discussing them helped them understand the text. Stress that making connections, asking questions, and reacting during reading can aid students' understanding of the selection.

References

Short, K. G., Harste, J. C., & Burke, C. (1996). *Creating classrooms for authors and inquirers* (2nd ed.). Portsmouth, NH: Heinemann.

Vaughan, J. L., & Estes, T. H. (1986). *Reading and reasoning beyond the primary grades.* Boston: Allyn & Bacon.

Sample Save the Last Word for Me for High School **Health**

✳ DIRECTIONS

As you read, make a light mark with your pencil next to three (3) statements in the passage that you either agree with, disagree with, connect with, or wish to comment about. When you finish reading, write each statement in one of the boxes below. Then write your comments below it. You might include questions or thoughts you have about each of the quotes. When you have finished, you will have an opportunity to discuss your comments with a small group of your classmates.

Coping with Loss

My First Quote, page _228_

Any loss requires change and that change can be stressful.

My Thoughts/Ideas/Questions about My First Quote

Change is hard when you don't choose it. That's what makes it stressful.

My Second Quote, page _229_

Hope operates through all five stages of grief.

My Thoughts/Ideas/Questions about My Second Quote

I think this is helpful to remember, especially when I am trying to help my girlfriend get over being hurt.

My Third Quote, page _230_

What helped me most was talking to my family.

My Thoughts/Ideas/Questions about My Third Quote

When my grandma died, it seemed that the only time I felt better was when I could be with my family and tell them how awful I was feeling.

Name _____ Date _____

 # Save the Last Word for Me

❋ DIRECTIONS

As you read, make a light mark with your pencil next to three (3) statements in the passage that you either agree with, disagree with, connect with, or wish to comment about. When you finish reading, write each statement in one of the boxes below. Then write your comments below it. You might include questions or thoughts you have about each of the quotes. When you have finished, you will have an opportunity to discuss your comments with a small group of your classmates.

Title: _____

My First Quote, page _____

My Thoughts/Ideas/Questions about My First Quote

My Second Quote, page _____

My Thoughts/Ideas/Questions about My Second Quote

My Third Quote, page _____

My Thoughts/Ideas/Questions about My Third Quote

Discussion Guide for Save the Last Word for Me

1. Choose someone to begin.

2. Have the first person read his or her first quote.

3. Moving around the circle, have each member of the group take a turn in commenting about the first person's quote.

4. When each person has had a chance to comment, the person who chose the quote may then share his or her comment about the quote. This may be a combination of what was written on the card as well as a response to what was said during the discussion.

5. Select another member of the group to read a quote.

6. Continue the reading and commenting until all quotes and comments have been made.

7. Remember that the person who shares his or her quote needs to be the **last** one to share his or her comments about it. In other words, "Save the last word for me!"

Say Something

FOCUS	TEXT	WHEN	WHY	HOW
Vocabulary	✓Narrative	Before Reading	✓Connecting ✓Questioning	Individual
Comprehension	✓Informational	✓During Reading	✓Synthesizing ✓Inferring	✓Small Group
✓Response		After Reading	Determining Importance	Whole Group

DESCRIPTION

Say Something (Short, Harste, & Burke, 1996) provides opportunities for students to respond to text. The strategy highlights the social nature of language by offering students the opportunity to share their thinking with a partner. At pre-selected stopping points in the reading, students make connection between the text and their own experiences and briefly discuss what the passage means to them. When using Say Something, students engage in proficient reader strategies by chunking text, posing questions, making predictions, and highlighting connections. Through the use of Say Something, students become more engaged in reading and aware of effective strategies to use when reading independently.

Procedure

1. Select a reading passage and stopping points within the passage. Paragraphs and sections of text with subheadings make good stopping points.
2. Invite students to choose a partner or designate partners.
3. Give each partner pair a copy of the text selection.
4. Invite each partner pair to decide how they will read the selection, silently or aloud.
5. To introduce the strategy, demonstrate the Say Something process with another student, using the first segment or two of the selected text.

6. When students appear to understand how to engage in the process, invite students to read to the next stopping point and Say Something to their partner about what they have read. Suggestions to help students successfully participate in Say Something are found on page 131. Emphasize that responses and interpretations are acceptable if the student can support the position.

7. When students finish the selection, conduct a discussion of the process. Create a list of the strategies students used while engaging in this strategy. Help students understand how they can use the strategies of predicting, connecting, questioning, inferring, and synthesizing when they are reading independently.

Reference

Short, K. G., Harste, J. C., & Burke, C. (1996). *Creating classrooms for authors and inquirers* (2nd ed.). Portsmouth, NH: Heinemann.

Say Something

When working with your partner, you might use the following ideas to form your comments.

* **I wonder . . .**

* **I was surprised that . . .**

* **It is interesting that . . .**

* **I think _____ will happen next . . .**

* **I don't understand . . .**

* **I think this means . . .**

* **This reminds me of . . .**

* **I especially liked . . .**

* **I am confused about . . .**

* **It surprised me when . . .**

* **I learned that . . .**

Select Two and Reflect (STAR)

FOCUS	TEXT	WHEN	WHY	HOW
✓Vocabulary	✓Narrative	Before Reading	✓Connecting Questioning	✓Individual
✓Comprehension	✓Informational	During Reading	Synthesizing Inferring	✓Small Group
✓Response		✓After Reading	Determining Importance	✓Whole Group

DESCRIPTION

Students are asked to choose two words from a selection that they have read and then explain in writing why those particular words were selected (Hoyt, 1999). Select Two and Reflect (STAR) encourages diverse thinking, honors individual responses, and invites students to react to words in a way that is personal and meaningful.

Procedure

1. Duplicate copies of the Select Two and Reflect (STAR) reproducible master on page 135 or adapt it to suit your needs or purposes.

2. Ask students to review a selection that has been read and to identify two interesting words. Do not, at this time, suggest any particular criteria for selecting the words.

3. After students have selected their words, ask for volunteers to share their words as you write them on the board or an overhead transparency.

4. Ask students to share why particular words were selected. Guide students to understand that some words were chosen because they were important in the selection. Other words were chosen because they reminded students of something in their lives, and sometimes words were selected because they were interesting in sound or possessed some other quality.

5. Make an overhead transparency of the reproducible master on page 135 so you can model STAR with two words. You might want to choose two volunteers to share their words and reasons. Write the words in the boxes and then write their reasons below. An example is given page 134.

6. Distribute copies of the STAR sheet to students after they have read a particular selection. Have students review the selection and write a word in each box. Then give students a few minutes to write why the words were selected.

7. Invite students to share their words and reasons in groups of three students.

8. Encourage whole group sharing after students have shared in their small groups. Expect and reinforce both the variety of words selected and the students' reasons for choosing them.

9. Model the process from time to time by completing a STAR sheet while students are completing theirs. Share your words and reasons with a small group of students or with the entire class.

Sample Select Two and Reflect (STAR) for Middle School Language Arts

✳ DIRECTIONS

Choose two words from the selection and explain why you chose them. You can also explain how they relate to your reading or your life.

Title: _____"Cheating Mr. Diskin"_____

money		dirt
Word 1		Word 2

Why Words Were Chosen

I chose money because the boys needed it to go to the show. They got the money by cheating. When they went to the show, they felt like dirt. Dirt is really low.

Reference

Hoyt, L. (1999). *Revisit, reflect, retell: Strategies for improving reading comprehension.* Portsmouth, NH: Heinemann.

Name _____ Date _____

 # Select Two and Reflect (STAR)

✳ DIRECTIONS

Choose two words from the selection and explain why you chose them. You can also explain how they relate to your reading or your life.

Title: _____

<table>
<tr><td style="border:1px solid; height:200px;"></td><td></td><td style="border:1px solid; height:200px;"></td></tr>
<tr><td align="center">Word 1</td><td></td><td align="center">Word 2</td></tr>
</table>

Why Words Were Chosen

_____

_____

_____

_____

_____

_____

_____

_____

Selective Reading Guide

FOCUS	TEXT	WHEN	WHY	HOW
✓Vocabulary	Narrative	Before Reading	Connecting Questioning	✓Individual
✓Comprehension	✓Informational	✓During Reading	Synthesizing Inferring	Small Group
Response		After Reading	✓Determining Importance	Whole Group

DESCRIPTION

The Selective Reading Guide (Cunningham & Shabloak, 1975) models for students how to identify important information in content area texts. Students are taught how mature readers make decisions about what to focus on while they read. Some portions of texts require more careful reading than other portions. The Selective Reading Guide strengthens students' abilities to be flexible in their reading (Tierney & Readence, 2005).

Procedure

1. Make an overhead transparency and duplicate copies of the Selective Reading Guide reproducible master on page 140. You may wish to adapt it to suit your needs or purposes.

2. Select a passage from a content area text that is new to your students.

3. Identify which concepts you wish your students to have mastered after reading the passage; that is, what should they know and what should they be able to do after the reading?

4. Make an overhead transparency of a page within the passage that includes examples of textual cues indicating importance, such as words in bold print or italics, subheadings, and words printed in different colors. You may wish to enlarge the copy of the passage to permit easier reading. Also consider highlighting the words that were in different colors in the original text. (See the reproducible master on page 140 for a more thorough list of cues.)

5. Discuss with students the kinds of difficulties they encounter when they attempt to thoroughly read content area texts. For example, they may describe their frustration in being unable to absorb all the information in the reading assignment or indicate it is difficult to stay focused when assignments are lengthy.

6. Distribute copies of the Selective Reading Guide. Explain to students that they are to self-monitor their reading by checking off the important characteristics as they find them.

7. Using the overhead transparencies of the passage and the Guide, read the passage or selection aloud and model for students how to attend to the important features in the text. For example, if you are modeling how to read a social studies text, show the students how to look for key dates, names, and places and tell them that generally the text will explain their importance either in the same sentence or in the following sentence. If you are modeling how to read a science text, demonstrate how to find the steps or stages the text describes by searching for words such as *first, next,* or *finally.* You may also wish to point out cause and effect words such as *because* and *therefore.* Also model how students may self-monitor their use of the Selective Reading Guide by checking off the steps as they complete them.

8. Direct students' attention to the assigned reading. Instruct students to silently read the passage and as they read to watch for the important features they have learned to identify. Also remind students to check off the steps to the strategy as they complete them.

9. When students are finished reading, ask for their feedback on the strategy. Discuss the situations for which this strategy would be most appropriate.

An additional example can be found on the CD-ROM accompanying this book.

References

Cunningham, R., & Shabloak, S. (1975). Selective reading guide-o-rama: The content teacher's best friend. *Journal of Reading, 18,* 380–382.

Tierney, R. J., & Readence, J. E. (2005). *Reading strategies and practices: A compendium* (6th ed.). Boston: Allyn & Bacon.

Sample Selective Reading Guide
for **Social Studies**

___✓___ I read the **HEADINGS** of the chapter sections and referred to them while I read the passage to help me remember the purpose of the reading.

___✓___ I read the **Subheadings** in the chapter and referred to them while I read to help me remember what each section was about.

___✓___ I paid special attention to words in color, in **bold print,** and in *italics,* and I watched for the meanings of those words in the sentences.

___✓___ I looked for key listing words such as *first, next,* and *because* to help me find important sequences of events or procedural steps to follow.

___✓___ I looked for proper nouns such as names of events, procedures, people, or places to help me know which are most important to recall.

Headings I Read

Africa's Climates
_____

Subheadings I Read

Different Climate Zones, Tropical Rain Forest Climate, Tropical Wet-and-Dry

Climate, Steppe Climate, Desert Climate, Mediterranean Climate

Words in Color, Bold Print, <u>Underlined</u>, or in *Italics* | **Meanings**

Words in Color, Bold Print, Underlined, or in *Italics*	Meanings
tropical rain forest climate	hot and rainy
tropical wet-and-dry climate	savannah, grassland
steppe climate	hot summers, cool winters
desert climate	extremely hot days, chilly nights (Sahara, Kalahari)
Mediterranean climate	cool & rainy winter, warm & dry summer

Sequence of Events or Procedural Steps to Follow

None
_____

Key Events, Procedures, People, Places, and Their Significance

Madagascar—tropical rain forest climate
Zambia—savannah
Sahara, Horn, Kalahari, & Namib—African deserts

Name _____   Date _____

Title _____   Pages _____

Selective Reading Guide

_____ I read the **<u>HEADINGS</u>** of the chapter sections and referred to them while I read the passage to help me remember the purpose of the reading.

_____ I read the **Subheadings** in the chapter and referred to them while I read to help me remember what each section was about.

_____ I paid special attention to words in color, in **bold print,** and in *italics,* and I watched for the meanings of those words in the sentences.

_____ I looked for key listing words such as *first, next,* and *because* to help me find important sequences of events or procedural steps to follow.

_____ I looked for proper nouns such as names of events, procedures, people, or places to help me know which are most important to recall.

Headings I Read

_____

Subheadings I Read

_____

Words in Color, in Bold Print, <u>Underlined</u>, or in *Italics*   **Meanings**

Sequence of Events or Procedural Steps to Follow

_____

Key Events, Procedures, People, Places, and Their Significance

Self-Monitoring Approach to Reading and Thinking (SMART)

FOCUS	TEXT	WHEN	WHY	HOW
Vocabulary	✓Narrative	Before Reading	Connecting ✓Questioning	✓Individual
✓Comprehension	✓Informational	✓During Reading	Synthesizing ✓Inferring	Small Group
Response		✓After Reading	Determining Importance	Whole Group

DESCRIPTION

The Self-Monitoring Approach to Reading and Thinking (SMART) (Buehl, 2001; Vaughan & Estes, 1986) is a during-reading and after-reading strategy that encourages students to develop an awareness of what they do and do not understand as they read. This self-monitoring strategy helps students think about their reading and be more aware of how it is proceeding. Students use a notation system during reading and a variety of fix-up strategies for difficult portions of the text after reading, thus enhancing their metacognition (awareness of one's own learning).

Procedure

1. Find a passage consisting of several paragraphs that is somewhat challenging for you. Make an overhead transparency of the passage. The passage may need to be enlarged for effective viewing by students.

2. Read aloud the first few sentences of the passage. If it makes sense to you, place a check mark (✓) in the margin using an overhead projector pen and say something like, "This makes sense to me. I feel like I really understand it." If it seems confusing, place a question mark (?) in the margin and say something like, "I'm not sure what this means. Maybe as I read on I will understand it better."

3. Continue modeling the use of the check mark (✓) and question mark (?) and comment on your reasons for using the marking system. You might say, "These marks will help me think about my reading and how well I am understanding what I am reading. Good readers know when they aren't understanding something, and they also know that they should try something else when they don't understand."

4. After completing the modeled reading for students, look at each question mark (?) and talk with students about how to make sense of those parts of the text. Sometimes just rereading the text helps a reader understand it. If this is the case for you, change the question mark (?) to a check mark (✓) in the margin. For other question-marked sections, talk about the problem. Why is this section difficult to understand? Is it the vocabulary? Is the language confusing? Do you know very little about the subject?

5. Ask students for their ideas of ways to help the text make sense. List these ideas on a blank overhead transparency or on the board as students offer them. Suggestions might be to paraphrase the text, use pictures, charts, or graphs to give clues to understanding, check the glossary or other references to determine the meaning of unknown or difficult words, look at other parts of the text such as the summary and review sections, and ask a teacher or another classmate for help. Take time to discuss how the various strategies may provide clues to meaning.

6. Introduce the passage students will be reading. After using an appropriate rereading strategy (e.g., Anticipation/Reaction Guide on page 1, Possible Sentences on page 103, K-W-L Plus on page 77), tell students to use a pencil to lightly mark the text using the check mark (✓) and question mark (?) system to help them monitor their reading.

7. Make copies of the SMART Strategy Log reproducible master on page 144. After students have read and marked their passages, have them work with a partner and discuss the sections marked with question marks (?). Have them use the SMART Strategy Log to record their reading processes. Remind students that if the problem is "something else," there is space provided to note the problem.

8. After completing the SMART Strategy Log, discuss with students the strategies that helped them work through problems with the text. Review or teach what they need to do when they don't understand what they are reading in subsequent lessons.

9. Have students complete the SMART Strategy Log from time to time to help make them more aware of ways to monitor their comprehension.

References

Buehl, D. (2001). *Classroom strategies for interactive learning* (2nd ed.). Newark, DE: International Reading Association.

Vaughan, J. L., & Estes, T. H. (1986). *Reading and reasoning beyond the primary grades.* Boston: Allyn & Bacon.

Sample SMART Strategy Log
for Intermediate **Mathematics**

✳ DIRECTIONS

After reading, find the page and paragraph of each question mark (?) in the margin of your text. Write them under the *Page/Paragraph* headings. Then look at each section of the text marked with a question mark (?). Ask yourself, *What's the Problem?* Check (✓) the things that may be problems or write your problem on the lines. Then try some fix-up strategies. Check (✓) those that you tried under the *What I Tried* column. Then think about how each strategy worked. Mark your responses in the *How It Worked* column with a check mark.

Page/Paragraph with "?"	*What's the Problem?*	*What I Tried*	*How It Worked*
__36__ / __3__	✓Difficult Word Confusing Sentence Don't Know Much About It _____ _____	✓Glossary Reread Text Pictures/Graphics Summarize Review Section Diagrams ✓Ask Someone Something Else	Great! I Get It! ✓It Helped OK Not Much Help
__38__ / __1__	Difficult Word ✓Confusing Sentence Don't Know Much About It _____ _____	Glossary ✓Reread Text Pictures/Graphics Summarize Review Section Diagrams Ask Someone Something Else	✓Great! I Get It! It Helped OK Not Much Help
__41__ / __2__	Difficult Word ✓Confusing Sentence Don't Know Much About It _____ _____	Glossary ✓Reread Text ✓Pictures/Graphics Summarize Review Section Diagrams Ask Someone Something Else	Great! I Get It! It Helped ✓OK Not Much Help
__43__ / __2__	Difficult Word Confusing Sentence ✓Don't Know Much About It ✓_Don't understand_ _____	Glossary ✓Reread Text ✓Pictures/Graphics Summarize Review Section ✓Diagrams Ask Someone Something Else	Great! I Get It! It Helped OK ✓Not Much Help

Name _____ Date _____

⊛ SMART Strategy Log

☀ DIRECTIONS

After reading, find the page and paragraph of each question mark (?) in the margin of your text. Write them under the *Page/Paragraph* headings. Then look at each section of the text marked with a question mark (?). Ask yourself, *What's the Problem?* Check (✓) the things that may be problems or write your problem on the lines. Then try some fix-up strategies. Check (✓) those that you tried under the *What I Tried* column. Then think about how each strategy worked. Mark your responses in the *How It Worked* column with a check mark.

Page/Paragraph with "?"	*What's the Problem?*	*What I Tried*	*How It Worked*
	Difficult Word	Glossary	Great! I Get It!
	Confusing Sentence	Reread Text	It Helped
	Don't Know Much About It	Pictures/Graphics	OK
/	_____	Summarize	Not Much Help
		Review Section	
___ ___	_____	Diagrams	
		Ask Someone	
		Something Else	

Page/Paragraph with "?"	*What's the Problem?*	*What I Tried*	*How It Worked*
	Difficult Word	Glossary	Great! I Get It!
	Confusing Sentence	Reread Text	It Helped
	Don't Know Much About It	Pictures/Graphics	OK
/	_____	Summarize	Not Much Help
		Review Section	
___ ___	_____	Diagrams	
		Ask Someone	
		Something Else	

Page/Paragraph with "?"	*What's the Problem?*	*What I Tried*	*How It Worked*
	Difficult Word	Glossary	Great! I Get It!
	Confusing Sentence	Reread Text	It Helped
	Don't Know Much About It	Pictures/Graphics	OK
/	_____	Summarize	Not Much Help
		Review Section	
___ ___	_____	Diagrams	
		Ask Someone	
		Something Else	

Page/Paragraph with "?"	*What's the Problem?*	*What I Tried*	*How It Worked*
	Difficult Word	Glossary	Great! I Get It!
	Confusing Sentence	Reread Text	It Helped
	Don't Know Much About It	Pictures/Graphics	OK
/	_____	Summarize	Not Much Help
		Review Section	
___ ___	_____	Diagrams	
		Ask Someone	
		Something Else	

Semantic Feature Analysis (SFA)

FOCUS	TEXT	WHEN	WHY	HOW
✓Vocabulary	✓Narrative	Before Reading	✓Connecting Questioning	✓Individual
Comprehension	✓Informational	During Reading	✓Synthesizing Inferring	✓Small Group
Response		✓After Reading	Determining Importance	✓Whole Group

DESCRIPTION

Semantic Feature Analysis (Berglund, 2002; Johnson & Pearson, 1984), is an instructional strategy that helps students discriminate the unique features of concepts or vocabulary. It uses a classification system in the form of a grid to help students determine semantic similarities and differences among closely related concepts.

Procedure

1. Using the reproducible master on page 148, create a transparency of the blank grid. Introduce the strategy by selecting a topic. It is best to introduce the SFA strategy to students by using a topic that is familiar to many of them, for example, Monsters.

2. List the words in the category down the left side of the grid. For the Monsters example, you might list *King Kong, Incredible Hulk, Dracula, Cookie Monster,* and *Godzilla.* Invite students to add additional monsters.

3. Across the top of the chart, list features shared by some of the words in the category. The features for Monsters might be *Hairy, Huge, Strong, Mean, Transforms.*

4. Consider each word in the category relative to the features listed across the top of the grid. A plus/minus (+/–) system or a numeric system (l=never, 2=some, 3=always) can be used to indicate feature possession. If the presence of the feature may be situational or not dichotomous, the numerical rating system might be more useful. A question mark (?) can signal the need for more information. A plus/minus rating (+/–) indicates that the feature may be present in differing degrees or at various times. In the Monster example, King Kong would probably receive pluses (+) for the features, *Hairy, Huge, Strong,* and *Mean,* but would receive a minus (–) for *Transforms.* Students should be encouraged to discuss and provide support for their ratings.

5. Complete the grid for each word in the category. You may need to add more features to the matrix in order to discriminate the differences among some of the words in the category. For example, if two of the monsters in the example have an identical pattern of features (pluses and minuses), then additional features would need to be added until the difference between the two is discriminated.

6. When the grid is complete, ask students to examine the similarities and differences among the words in the category selected. Discuss some of their conclusions. Using the pattern of pluses and minuses, encourage students to create a summary statement regarding some of the words in the grid. For example, the summary of knowledge about Monsters might go something like this, *"King Kong, Dracula,* and *Godzilla* are all examples of monsters who are strong. Most monsters are huge, but not all monsters are mean."*

Sample Semantic Feature Analysis for Intermediate Grade Reading

Harry Potter Character Comparison

Words	Loyal	Foolhardy	Clever	Egocentric	Idealistic	Opportunistic					
Harry	+	+	+	−	+	+					
Hermione	+	+	+	−	+	−					
Ron	+	+	−	−	+	−					
Dudley	−	?	−	+	−	−					
Snape	+	−	+	+	−	+					

Summary: The three friends, Harry, Hermione, and Ron, were all loyal to each other and all were also foolhardy and idealistic at some point in the story.

References

Berglund, R. L. (2002). Semantic feature analysis in B. J. Guzzetti (Ed.), *Literacy in America: An encyclopedia of history, theory, and practice* (pp. 566–572). Santa Barbara, CA: ABC-CLIO.

Johnson, D. D., & Pearson, P. D, (1984). *Teaching reading vocabulary* (2nd ed.). New York: Holt, Rinehart, and Winston.

Sample Semantic Feature Analysis
for High School **Earth Science**

Rivers and River Characteristics

Words	Features	Caused by Erosion	Caused by Deposition	Old	Mature	Young							
Waterfalls	+	−	−	−	+								
Rapids	+	−	−	−	+								
Wide Flood Plain	+	+	+	+/−	−								
U-Shape Valley	+	−	−	−	+								
Meander	+	+	+	+	−								
Oxbow	+	−	+	−	−								
Yazoo Stream	−	+	+	−	−								
No Flood Plain	−	−	−	−	+								
Back Swamp	−	+	+	−	−								
Sand Bar	−	+	+	+	−								

Summary: Waterfalls, rapids, wide flood plains, u-shaped valleys, meanders, and oxbows are all caused by erosion, while yazoo streams, back swamps, and sand bars are caused by deposition.

Name _____ Date _____

 # Semantic Feature Analysis (SFA)

Features

Words

Summary:

Sticky Notes

FOCUS	TEXT	WHEN	WHY	HOW
Vocabulary	✓Narrative	Before Reading	✓Connecting ✓Questioning	✓Individual
✓Comprehension	✓Informational	✓During Reading	✓Synthesizing Inferring	Small Group
✓Response		✓After Reading	✓Determining Importance	Whole Group

DESCRIPTION

Sticky Notes (Daniels & Zemelman, 2004; Harvey & Goudvis, 2000; Hoyt, 2002) encourage students to monitor their thinking while reading by jotting down quick notes and sticking them on the pages of the text that prompted their thoughts. Students can jot down quick comments, write questions, make predictions and connections, or mark an interesting phrase or sentence in the text. Sticky Notes become a record of students' thinking that can later be used for review, discussion, and assessment.

Procedure

1. Choose a passage from a text to read aloud and provide copies so that students can follow along with you. Explain that you will be stopping while reading to write down your thinking on Sticky Notes.

2. Begin reading the text aloud and stop at a point where you can share a personal connection, ask a question, make a prediction, or express appreciation of the author's use of language. For example, while reading aloud from the first chapter of *Fever 1793* (Anderson, 2000), you could stop after a mosquito bites Mattie. Ask students if they know anything about mosquitos spreading diseases. Some students may mention the West Nile Virus. Since Mattie was bitten by a mosquito, you may want to make a prediction that Mattie will become sick with yellow fever. On a Sticky Note, write down your prediction, read it aloud to students, then place it on the page to mark the spot in the text to show your thinking. Continue reading and stopping to share your written thoughts on Sticky Notes.

3. As you continue reading aloud, elicit students' thoughts. Model how to jot down their responses on the Sticky Notes using a chart, overhead transparency, or the board.

4. After modeling several examples, provide time for students to practice individually recording their thinking on Sticky Notes.

5. Invite students to share their Sticky Notes with a partner or use them in a whole class discussion. You might ask students to place their Sticky Notes on chart paper after reading a selection of text or use the reproducible on page 151. Responses can be organized into like categories and used to engage students in discussion. Possible categories might include predictions, connections, questions, and interesting passages.

6. With informational text, you can demonstrate how to mark a photo or illustration in the text with a question. Students can be encouraged to record their senses to help comprehend text. For example, while reading an article in *National Geographic* titled "Thailand's Urban Giants," students could be asked to write what they saw, heard, smelled, tasted, and felt about the inhumane treatment of the elephants.

7. Upon completion of the reading, students should have a collection of Sticky Notes that can be stored in a notebook for later discussion and review.

References

Anderson, H. L. (2000). *Fever 1793.* New York, NY: Aladdin.

Daniels, H., & Zemelman, S. (2004). *Subjects matter: Every teacher's guide to content-area reading.* Portsmouth, NH: Heinemann.

Harvey, S., & Goudvis, A. (2000). *Strategies that work.* Portland, ME: Stenhouse.

Hoyt, L. (2002). *Make it real: Strategies for success with informational texts.* Portsmouth, NH: Heinemann.

Name _____ Date _____

 **Sticky Notes Record Sheet**

Text or Selection _____

Pages _____
Pages _____
Pages _____

Story Map

FOCUS	TEXT	WHEN	WHY	HOW
Vocabulary	✓Narrative	Before Reading	Connecting Questioning	✓Individual
✓Comprehension	Informational	During Reading	✓Synthesizing Inferring	✓Small Group
Response		✓After Reading	✓Determining Importance	Whole Group

DESCRIPTION

Story mapping (Beck & McKeown, 1981) provides a graphic representation of a story or novel by displaying the key story elements. By completing a story map and identifying the plot, characters, setting, problem, resolution, and theme, students can demonstrate their comprehension of the common elements of a story and create a visual aid to enable them to better remember a story (Buehl, 2001). Two types of Story Map reproducible masters are provided on pages 156 and 157.

Procedure

1. Select two short stories that clearly illustrate the common story elements such as plot, characters, setting, problem, resolution, and theme. One story will be for you to model the strategy to students and the other story will be for students to read and map on their own. There is an example of a completed story map on page 155.

2. Read the story to the class that you will use to model the Story Map strategy.

3. Make an overhead transparency and duplicate copies of one of the Story Map reproducible masters or adapt it to suit your needs or purposes.

4. Model for students how to complete a story map. Discuss with students the basic outline of the story in terms of its common elements. As students describe the plot, characters, setting, problem, solution, and theme, you could model how to simplify their descriptions and write them in the appropriate places on the map. You may need to restate students' descriptions to simplify them. If so, think aloud how to keep the descriptions brief and concise. For example, if a student described the setting of the sample story "Mr. Diskin" in a long paragraph, such as, "The story takes place in the town of Jonesville, USA. The two main settings are in the Diskins' house and in the dollar store that's downtown," you would model the appropriateness of writing in short phrases instead. For example, "Jonesville, USA; the Diskins' house; the downtown dollar store."

5. Reproduce and distribute copies of the Story Map and the second short story. Explain to students that they are to first read the story and then complete the story map. Assure them that it is appropriate to go back and reread parts of the story to help them identify the common elements.

6. When students are finished completing the story maps on their own, ask them to share their story maps in small groups. Have them discuss how decisions were made and provide opportunities for students to explain why they agree or disagree with one another's story map descriptions. For example, in a story about a boy drowning in a river, one student may say that the river can be considered to be a character and another student may disagree. In a story about Holocaust survivors, one student may see a theme of the strength of family love and another student may see a theme of persecution.

7. Give students opportunities to design their own story maps to reflect the nature of the stories they are reading. For example, students reading a story about ancient Egypt may wish to create a story map in the shape of a pyramid. Students reading a story about a haunted house may wish to create a story map in the shape of a house.

8. As an extension activity, discuss with students how they may use story maps to help them organize their own writing.

References

Beck, I., & McKeown, M. (1981). Developing questions that promote comprehension: The story map. *Language Arts, 58,* 913–918.

Buehl, D. (2001). *Classroom strategies for interactive learning* (2nd ed.). Newark, DE: International Reading Association.

Sample Story Map
for Middle School **Literature**

Title
Mr. Diskin

Setting
Jonesville, USA; the Diskin's house; the downtown dollar store

Characters
Mr. Diskin, Mrs. Diskin, their daughter Irma, and the owner of the downtown dollar store

Problem
Irma wants to be treated like a grown up, but she is only 13.

Events

Irma lies about her age to get a job at the downtown dollar store.

⇩

Mr. & Mrs. Diskin wonder why Irma suddenly has so much money.
They are worried and curious.

⇩

Irma hears her parents talking and has to decide whether to tell her boss and her parents the truth.

⇩

When Mrs. Diskin goes shopping, she goes to the store Irma is working in and finds out the truth before Irma has chance to tell her.

Solution Irma apologizes to her boss and her parents for lying and explains she wanted to feel more grown up. Her boss hires her to babysit, and her parents decide not to ground her.

 **Story Map**

Title

Setting

Characters

Problem

Events

⇩

⇩

⇩

Solution

Based on Beck and McKeown (1981). From Jerry L. Johns and Roberta L. Berglund, *Strategies for Content Area Learning* (2nd ed.). Copyright © 2006 by Kendall/Hunt Publishing Company (1-800-247-3458, ext. 4). May be reproduced for noncommercial educational purposes. www.kendallhunt.com/readingresources.html

 # Story Map

Title: _____

_____

Major Characters: _____

Minor Characters: _____

_____

Climax:

Setting:

Events: Rising Action

6. _____
5. _____
4. _____
3. _____
2. _____
1. _____

Falling Action

7. _____
8. _____
9. _____
10. _____

Conflict:

Resolution:

Theme:

Text Dialogue

FOCUS	TEXT	WHEN	WHY		HOW
Vocabulary	✓Narrative	Before Reading	✓Connecting	✓Questioning	✓Individual
✓Comprehension	Informational	During Reading	✓Synthesizing	✓Inferring	✓Small Group
✓Response		✓After Reading	Determining Importance		Whole Group

DESCRIPTION

The purpose of Text Dialogue (Lenski, Wham, Johns, & Caskey, 2006) is to help students process and reflect on what they have read by summarizing, interpreting, and evaluating. Students complete the Text Dialogue after reading and then interact with their peers and teacher to further discuss the reading. Instead of requiring comprehension questions to be answered or book reports to be written following a reading assignment, the Text Dialogue strategy may be assigned as an alternate means of demonstrating comprehension. This strategy is an adaptation of the Book Dialogue strategy, created by Miller (1994) as a tool for students in a college developmental reading course to improve their skills of reflection and response.

Procedure

1. Make an overhead transparency and duplicate copies of the Text Dialogue reproducible master on page 162. You may wish to adapt it to suit your needs or purposes.

2. Choose text selections that students will be asked to read. Choose one passage from the text to use for modeling the strategy and choose another passage for independent student practice.

3. Use the sample Text Dialogue on page 161 to demonstrate for students how the strategy works. Model for them how to complete the sheet. First, complete the information at the top of the form, and then think aloud as you write a summary of the most important ideas. Next, think aloud as you write your own interpretation of the passage. Stress to students that their well-thought-out reasoning is more important than trying to find the "right" answer. Finally, think aloud as you evaluate the reading. Address critical issues such as accuracy, your level of interest, whether the style of writing is engaging, and the likelihood that you would seek out either more information on this topic or more literature by this author. In this final step, emphasize to students that it is their opportunity to be the critics. Explain that it is important for students to support their opinions with specific reasons.

4. Distribute blank copies of the Text Dialogue form, instruct students to read the selected passages, and have them complete the form after they have finished reading.

5. Assign each student a partner. Instruct the partners to discuss their text dialogues in the context of the following guiding questions:

   - In what areas did you and your partner disagree? Why?
   - What specific examples can you use to support your opinions?
   - How were your and your partner's interpretations similar and different?
   - How were your and your partner's evaluations similar and different?
   - How did making connections help you understand the material?

   Suggest that the partners keep notes of the outcome of their discussion so that they will be prepared to share their comments with the class.

6. Once the partners have finished their discussions, bring the whole class together to share their thoughts.

References

Lenski, S. D., Wham, M. A., Johns, J. L., & Caskey, M. M. (2006). *Reading and learning strategies: Middle grades through high school.* (3rd ed.). Dubuque, IA: Kendall/Hunt.

Miller, E. F. (1994). Book dialogues. *Journal of Reading, 37,* 415–416.

Sample Text Dialogue
for High School **Literature**

Title: _Awesome Women_

Author: _A. Love-Green_

Type of Text: _Biography_

What I thought was most important:

> Throughout history, there have been strong, smart, independent women who were persecuted because they were different. Some were young, some were old, some were rich, some were poor. They all were punished for their strengths. Even today, some women are under suspicion because they don't fit society's ideas of how women should look, think, act, and live.

My interpretation:

> This means to me that it is okay to be different and that I should not be so quick to decide that I do not like someone just because she acts or looks differently from me. If more women had the courage to be themselves, and if people weren't so judgmental, the world would be a better place.

What it meant to me:

> This text was very meaningful to me because I like to read about good female role models. I could tell that Love-Green really worked hard to find accurate information about the women in her book. It was helpful because it gave me ideas of women to write about the next time I have to do a research paper.

Name _____ Date _____

 **Text Dialogue**

Title: _____

Author: _____

Type of Text: _____

What I thought was most important:

┌───┐
│   │
│   │
│   │
│   │
│   │
│   │
└───┘

My interpretation:

┌───┐
│   │
│   │
│   │
│   │
│   │
│   │
└───┘

What it meant to me:

┌───┐
│   │
│   │
│   │
│   │
│   │
│   │
└───┘

Vocabulary Self-Collection Strategy (VSS)

FOCUS	TEXT	WHEN	WHY	HOW
✓Vocabulary	✓Narrative	✓Before Reading	Connecting Questioning	Individual
Comprehension	✓Informational	During Reading	Synthesizing ✓Inferring	✓Small Group
Response		✓After Reading	✓Determining Importance	✓Whole Group

DESCRIPTION

The Vocabulary Self-Collection Strategy (Haggard, 1986; Ruddell & Shearer, 2002) is a simple, powerful technique to help promote long term vocabulary growth in all content areas. Central to the strategy is the self-selection of words to be learned. Students identify possible vocabulary in reading assignments to explore and learn through conversations with other students and the entire class. The strategy generates an interest in words that can help strengthen vocabulary growth.

Procedure

1. Make a transparency of the Vocabulary Self-Collection reproducible on page 165 to help introduce the VSS. You may also want to make copies for each student.

2. Model each of the areas using the transparency on an overhead projector. You might say the following.

   I have reviewed the assignment you are about to read, and I would like to nominate one word that I think we should learn. The word is labor force. It is found on page 95 in this sentence: The United States labor force totaled 127 million in 1992 and is expected to reach over 150 million in 2006. [Write the appropriate information on the transparency.] I looked the word up in the glossary and found it meant the number of people over the age of 16 who are actively seeking work. I found the meaning in the glossary, so I will check glossary on the transparency. The word is important to learn for at least two reasons. First, the assignment deals with jobs of the future and what the labor force will look like. Second, the text shares information about how the labor force will be changing by the time many of you are making career choices. You will now be asked to use the sheet I've shared to nominate a word that our class should learn.

3. Divide the class into groups of two to five students.

4. Have students go through the reading assignment and identify one word they believe the entire class should learn. The word should be important in the reading selection. The reproducible on page 165 will help guide students through the process. As students work, circulate among the groups to offer encouragement and assistance as needed. Each group should decide which word to select and note the page and paragraph where it is found. They should then write the sentence containing the word, determine its meaning, and generate reasons why the word should be learned. Provide sufficient time for students to complete the sheet for the nominated word.

5. Call the groups together and have them present their nominated word to the entire class. One person from each group
   - identifies the word and reads the sentence in which the word is used.
   - offers the group's consensus regarding the meaning of the word.
   - provides reasons why the word is important enough for the class to learn.

6. As each group shares, facilitate the discussion, write the nominated words on the board with consensus meanings, and encourage additional clarifications of the words as needed.

7. After all words are presented, the class should eliminate duplications, words already known, and words students do not want to learn.

8. The resulting words and their definitions can be written on the reproducible found on page 166—Words Chosen for Vocabulary Self-Collection. The resulting list "focuses on words that students want to learn, that are important to them, and about which they have expressed interest and curiosity" (Ruddell & Shearer, 2002, p. 353).

9. Facilitate further learning in subsequent class sessions through discussion, Semantic Mapping (see page 83), Semantic Feature Analysis (see page 145), Concept Circles (see page 21), and other interactive word activities.

10. The reproducible on page 167 can be used by individual students to develop their unique vocabulary notebooks.

References

Haggard, M. R. (1986). The vocabulary self-collection strategy: Using student interest and world knowledge to enhance vocabulary growth. *Journal of Reading, 29,* 634–642.

Ruddell, M. R., & Shearer, B. A. (2002). "Extraordinary," "tremendous," "exhilarating," "magnificant": Middle school at-risk students become avid word learners with the Vocabulary Self-Collection Strategy (VSS). *Journal of Adolescent & Adult Literacy, 45,* 352–363.

Name _____ Date _____

★ Vocabulary Self-Collection

Names of Group Members _____

Title of Selection or Text _____

Word Selected _____ Page/Paragraph _____

Word in Sentence _____

What does the word mean?

_____

_____

_____

We used _____ Context

_____ Glossary

_____ Dictionary

_____ Other _____

Why we think the word is important to learn.

_____

_____

_____

_____

_____

Name _____ Date _____

Words Chosen for
Vocabulary Self-Collection

Title of Text or Selection _____

Pages _____

Word	**Meaning**
1. _____	_____
	_____
	_____
2. _____	_____
	_____
	_____
3. _____	_____
	_____
	_____
4. _____	_____
	_____
	_____
5. _____	_____
	_____
	_____
6. _____	_____
	_____
	_____
7. _____	_____
	_____
	_____
8. _____	_____
	_____
	_____

My Personally Selected
Vocabulary Words

Word	Meaning
1. _____	_____
	_____
	_____
2. _____	_____
	_____
	_____
3. _____	_____
	_____
	_____
4. _____	_____
	_____
	_____
5. _____	_____
	_____
	_____
6. _____	_____
	_____
	_____
7. _____	_____
	_____
	_____
8. _____	_____
	_____
	_____

Word Map

FOCUS	TEXT	WHEN	WHY	HOW
✓Vocabulary	✓Narrative	Before Reading	Connecting Questioning	✓Individual
Comprehension	✓Informational	✓During Reading	Synthesizing Inferring	✓Small Group
Response		✓After Reading	✓Determining Importance	Whole Group

DESCRIPTION

A Word Map (Schwartz & Raphael, 1985) is a graphic representation of the definition of a word. The map contains the word, the category to which it belongs, some of its essential characteristics, and some examples. These elements compose a good definition. Word Maps help students understand the attributes and characteristics of a word's meaning. Due to the time it takes to complete the map, the Word Map graphic organizer should be used for key concept words. It is most effectively used with nouns.

Procedure

1. Make a transparency of the Word Map graphic organizer on page 172 and display it on an overhead projector. Tell students that this type of map can help them think about what they need to know in order to understand a new word.

2. Model the use of the map by choosing a well-understood concept and inviting the class to participate in completing the map with you. For example, the chosen word might be *ice cream*. Write *ice cream* in the box in the center of the transparency. Ask, "What is it?" Students might say, "food" or "dessert." Write one of the responses in the proper place on the transparency. Then ask, "What makes ice cream different from other foods or dairy products?" Properties might include *frozen, sweet, creamy, melts.* List these properties in the proper place on the transparency. Finally, ask students for some kinds of ice cream they know. Examples could be *chocolate, strawberry,* and *vanilla.* Write these words in the appropriate place on the transparency.

3. Duplicate the Word Map reproducible master on page 172 and distribute copies to students.

4. Present a key term or concept from the lesson.

5. Invite students to work individually or in pairs to complete a map for the key concept word. They may wish to use their textbooks, their own background knowledge, or a combination of resources to assist them.

6. When the maps are completed, have students share some of their ideas and then write a definition of the key concept word. The definition should include the category of the word, some properties or characteristics, and specific examples. For instance, the definition of ice cream might be, "Ice cream is a dessert that is frozen, tastes sweet, is creamy, and melts if it is left at room temperature or when it is eaten. Chocolate, strawberry, and vanilla are three popular kinds of ice cream."

7. Additional Word Maps are found on pages 173–174.

An additional example can be found on the CD-ROM accompanying this book.

Reference

Schwartz, R. M., & Raphael, T. E. (1985). Concept of definition: A key to improving students' vocabulary. *The Reading Teacher, 39,* 198–205.

Sample Word Map
for **Algebra**

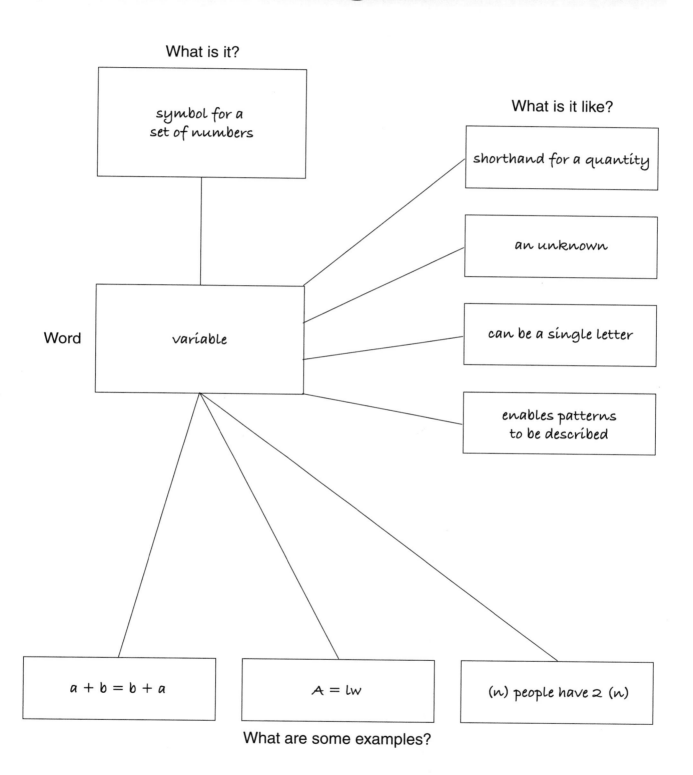

What is it?

symbol for a
set of numbers

What is it like?

shorthand for a quantity

an unknown

can be a single letter

enables patterns
to be described

Word

variable

$a + b = b + a$

$A = lw$

(n) people have 2 (n)

What are some examples?

 # Word Map

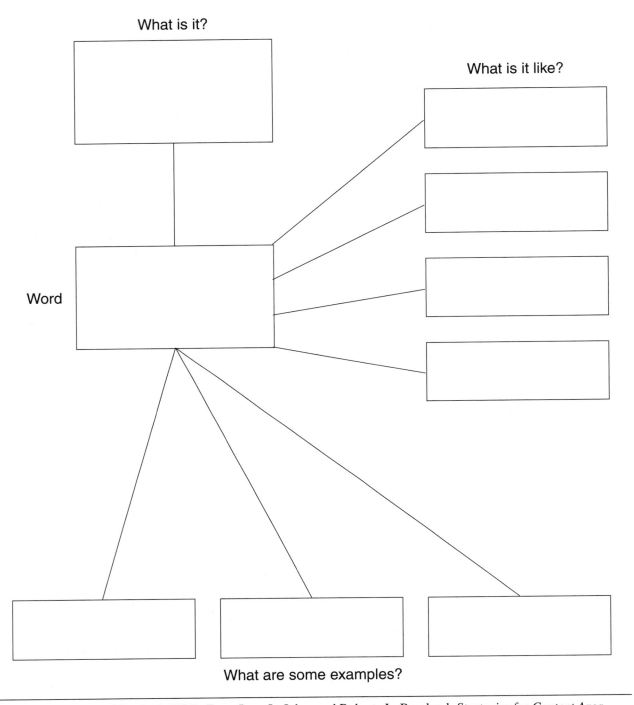

What is it?

What is it like?

Word

What are some examples?

Name _____   Date _____

 **Word Map**

Category
What is it?

Properties
What is it like?

Word

Comparison

Examples

Based on Schwartz and Raphael (1985). From Jerry L. Johns and Roberta L. Berglund, *Strategies for Content Area Learning* (2nd ed.). Copyright © 2006 by Kendall/Hunt Publishing Company (1-800-247-3458, ext. 4). May be reproduced for noncommercial educational purposes. www.kendallhunt.com/readingresources.html

Name _____ Date _____

⊛ Word Map

Definition or Synonym	Antonym

Word

Use it in a sentence	Draw a picture

Based on Schwartz and Raphael (1985). From Jerry L. Johns and Roberta L. Berglund, *Strategies for Content Area Learning* (2nd ed.). Copyright © 2006 by Kendall/Hunt Publishing Company (1-800-247-3458, ext. 4). May be reproduced for noncommercial educational purposes. www.kendallhunt.com/readingresources.html

Word Sort

FOCUS	TEXT	WHEN	WHY	HOW
✓Vocabulary	Narrative	✓Before Reading	✓Connecting Questioning	Individual
✓Comprehension	✓Informational	During Reading	Synthesizing ✓Inferring	✓Small Group
Response		✓After Reading	Determining Importance	Whole Group

DESCRIPTION

In a Word Sort (Gillet & Kita, 1979), students classify words into categories based on their prior knowledge and experiences. The Word Sort strategy is derived from Taba's (1967) List-Group-Label strategy and is based on the belief that placing words into categories helps students to organize and remember vocabulary and concepts. There are two types of Word Sorts, open and closed. In a Closed Word Sort, the categories are predetermined. Closed Word Sorts are generally easier for students because all of the words are clustered under the selected headings that are given to them. In an Open Word Sort, students are invited to consider characteristics and meanings of the words and then cluster the words into categories that they select. Some of the words in the sort can be used for category headings, or students can create new headings. Word Sorts can be used before reading to elicit background knowledge and set purposes for reading or as an after-reading activity to consolidate and refine new learning. Inviting students to sort the same words both before and after reading encourages reflection and refinement of the major concepts in the lesson. This sorting provides a cross-checking experience that can enhance metacognition (awareness of one's own learning).

Procedure

1. Select 15–20 vocabulary words that are important for understanding the lesson. Be sure to include some familiar words along with the new words students will be encountering.

2. Write the words on note cards. Make identical sets of cards for each small group. (An alternate idea is to write the words on the reproducible master on page 178 and have students cut them apart for sorting.)

3. Cluster students into groups of 3–5 students, giving each group a set of the note cards containing the vocabulary words.

4. If it is a Closed Word Sort, inform the students of the categories that you have selected. If it is an Open Word Sort, tell the students to read the words and cluster them into categories that make sense to them. They need to be able to defend their classifications.

5. Allow students about ten minutes to complete the sort. After students have completed the Word Sort, invite groups to rotate around the classroom, examining how others have clustered the words, or have them share their classifications orally.

6. As students read or experience the lesson, direct them to reclassify their words based on their expanding knowledge of the subject area.

7. Invite students to share their reflections. Were their initial classifications correct? Did they make changes? If so, why?

References

Gillet, J., & Kita, M. J. (1979). Words, kids and categories. *The Reading Teacher, 32,* 538–542.

Taba, H. (1967). *Teacher's handbook for elementary social studies.* Reading, MA: Addison-Wesley.

Sample Open Word Sort
for Middle School Science

✳ DIRECTIONS

Below are some words that you will find in your lesson. Cut them apart and arrange them in categories according to their meanings. You must be able to justify the reasons for your decisions.

The Sun
_____
(topic)

solar flare	solar composition	magnetic storm
solar structure	helium	photosphere
aurora	core	solar wind
atmosphere	hydrogen	sunspot
corona	prominence	chromosphere
solar activities	solar eclipse	nuclear fusion

Sample Closed Word Sort
for Intermediate Grade Social Studies

✳ DIRECTIONS

Arrange each of the words below into one of the categories in bold type.

Anasazi Indians
_____
(topic)

Who They Were		**What They Did**		**Where They Lived**
ancient ones	nomadic	canyon	invaders	cliff palace
kiva	metates	abode	cliffs	stone masons
hunters	mesa	excavation	swallows	preserve

177

Name _____ Date _____

 **Word Sort**

_____

(topic)

※ **DIRECTIONS**

Below are some words that you will find in your lesson. Cut them apart and arrange them in categories according to their meanings. You must be able to justify the reasons for your decisions.

Appendix A
Informational Text Structures

Overview

This appendix contains the five basic informational text structures that are found in content area materials. Included are

- A succinct overview of the five text structures.
- Common signal or cue words for each of the text patterns.
- An example for each text structure.
- A basic lesson plan for teaching text structure and the use of related graphic organizers.
- Reproducible graphic organizers for each text structure.

Appendix B
Websites for Resources and Further Learning

Overview

This appendix contains websites for

- Content Areas
- Strategies, Games, Graphic Organizers, and Resources

Appendix B is found on the CD-ROM accompanying this book.

Informational Text Structures

Text Pattern	Description	Signal Words	Graphic Organizer
Description Main Idea/Details	Key concept or idea and details about characteristics, attributes, features, actions, examples	For instance, for example, to begin with, that is, also, such as, in fact, along with, in addition, in other words, as, specifically, furthermore, most important	
Time Order/ Sequence	Information is given in chronological or numerical order	First, second, third, on (date), at, not, long after, now, during, next, then, last, later, when, before, earlier	
Compare/Contrast	How two or more things are alike and/or different	However, on the other hand, but, yet, as well as, like/unlike, in contrast, similarly, on the contrary, likewise, although, instead, otherwise, while, rather, most, same, as opposed to	
Cause/Effect	Ideas, events, or facts are presented with effects or facts that happen as a result	Because, if/then, since, therefore, consequently, as a result, nevertheless, thus, subsequently, so, for this reason, due to, this led to, so that	
Problem/Solution	A problem is stated with one or more solutions offered	Problem is, question is, dilemma is, if/then, because, so that, question/answer, conclude, a solution is, propose that	

From Jerry L. Johns and Roberta L. Berglund, *Strategies for Content Area Learning* (2nd ed.). Copyright © 2006 by Kendall/Hunt Publishing Company (1-800-247-3458, ext. 4). May be reproduced for noncommercial educational purposes. www.kendallhunt.com/readingresources.html

Signal Words for Text Patterns

DESCRIPTION MAIN IDEAS/ DETAILS	TIME ORDER/ SEQUENCE	COMPARE/ CONTRAST	CAUSE/ EFFECT	PROBLEM/ SOLUTION
For instance	First	However	Because	Problem is
For example	Second	On the other hand	If/then	Question is
To begin with	Third	But	Since	Dilemma is
That is	On (date)	Yet	Therefore	If/then
Also	At	As well as	Consequently	Because
Such as	Not long after	Like/unlike	As a result	So that
In fact	Now	In contrast	Nevertheless	Question/answer
Along with	During	On the contrary	Thus	Conclude
In addition to	Next	Likewise	Subsequently	A solution is
In other words	Then	Although	So	Propose that
As	Last	Instead	For this reason	
Specifically	Later	Otherwise	Due to	
Furthermore	When	While	This led to	
Most important	Before	Rather	So that	
	Earlier	Most		
		Same		
		As opposed to		

Text Structures and Examples

Description

Main Idea/Supporting Details

A key concept or idea is presented followed by more information about the concept or idea.

Example

Main Idea   The monarchs themselves were regularly in France.

Details   William I spent half his reign in Normandy. William II and Henry I also spent half of their reigns there, as did Henry II, who lived there for as many as twenty years.

Time Order/Sequence

Information is given in the order that it happened or in a sequence.

Example

By the thirteenth century, English was the dominant language in the Lowland south and east. By 1400 the Scottish dialect had evolved. By the 1500s, it was clear that a standard dialect was emerging throughout the land.

Compare/Contrast

Information shows how two or more things are alike and/or different.

Example

Two variations of the English language emerged, Middle English and Standard English. Both were used throughout the land, but different regions began to use one or the other predominantly.

In Middle English, all dialects were equal and written language contained a wide range of forms, each being acceptable. No one minded if a writer spelled a word differently in different parts of the same text.

With the rise of Standard English, agreement arose about how things should be said and written. As more people became able to read and write, the need for norms grew. There was a growing sense of shared usage.

Cause/Effect

Ideas, events, or facts are presented with things that happen as a result.

Example

As more people became able to read and write, the need for a standardized language became apparent.

Problem/Solution

A problem is given and one or more solutions are offered.

Example

In the 1500s, there was huge amount of variation in how language was used and written. As more people learned to read and write, the variation in language usage hindered communication. In order to solve the problem, people needed to work together to develop a common style. Many people needed to interact regularly and frequently.

Text Structure/Graphic Organizers Lesson Plan

Description

This strategy makes use of graphic organizers, a powerful means of visually representing ideas and information. Graphic organizers provide students with a framework for recording their notes, which can also be used for review and study. Graphic organizers serve purposes similar to outlining, but with more flexibility.

Procedure

1. Select a passage that you want students to read.
2. Select the graphic organizer(s) to suit your text structure. Provide copies to students (see pages 185-193).
3. Explain to students that you will be modeling the use of graphic organizers to help them understand how the information is organized, thus promoting better comprehension.
4. Explain the five main patterns for organizing content texts: description, sequence, compare/contrast, cause/effect, and problem/solution. Show examples of each type.
5. Model how to use the graphic organizers using examples from your content area materials by reading the text and identifying important information.
6. Ask students to read another text selection and fill in the graphic organizer.
7. Discuss the information students record on the completed graphic organizer and how they might use it for review and study.

From Jerry L. Johns and Roberta L. Berglund, *Strategies for Content Area Learning* (2nd ed.). Copyright © 2006 by Kendall/Hunt Publishing Company (1-800-247-3458, ext. 4). May be reproduced for noncommercial educational purposes. www.kendallhunt.com/readingresources.html

Main Idea and Supporting Details Text Pattern

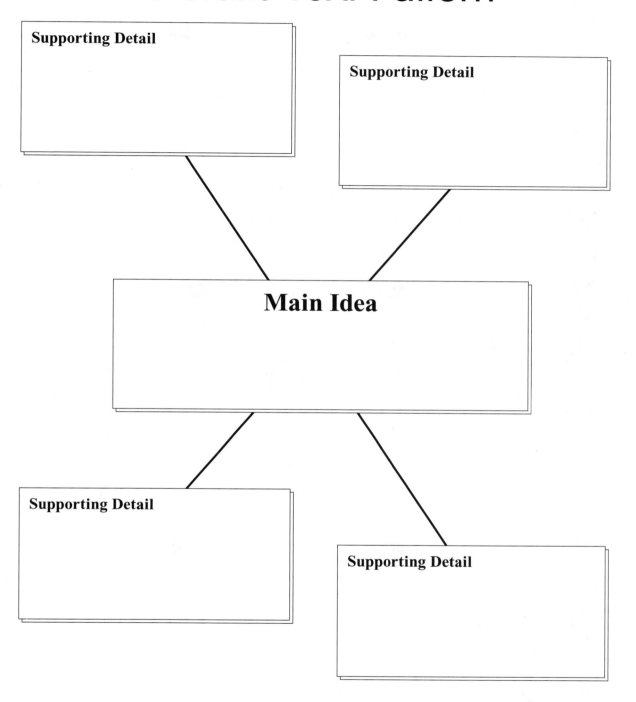

Supporting Detail

Supporting Detail

Main Idea

Supporting Detail

Supporting Detail

Main Idea and Supporting Details Text Pattern

Main Idea

Details

Main Idea and Supporting Details Text Pattern

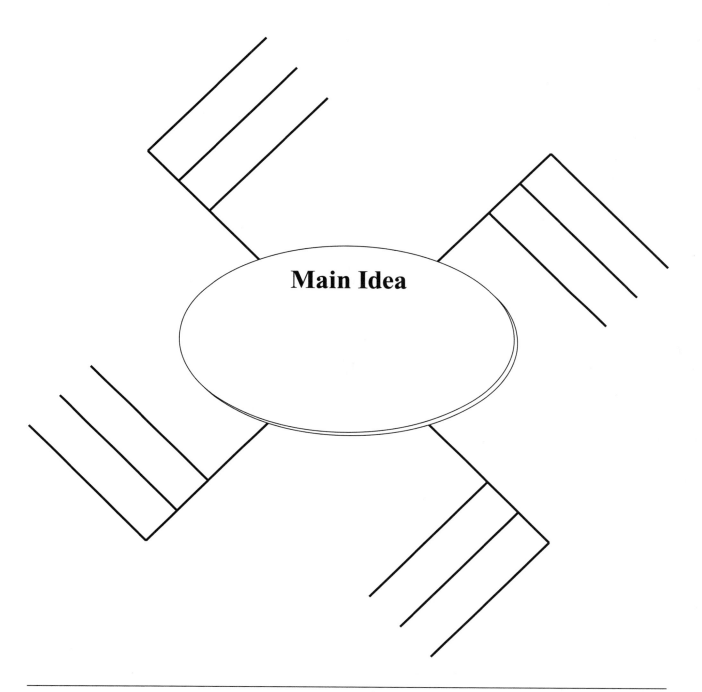

Main Idea

Sequence of Events Text Pattern

```
┌────────────────────────────────────────┐
│                                        │
└────────────────────────────────────────┘
                    ⬇
┌────────────────────────────────────────┐
│                                        │
└────────────────────────────────────────┘
                    ⬇
┌────────────────────────────────────────┐
│                                        │
└────────────────────────────────────────┘
                    ⬇
┌────────────────────────────────────────┐
│                                        │
└────────────────────────────────────────┘
                    ⬇
┌────────────────────────────────────────┐
│                                        │
└────────────────────────────────────────┘
                    ⬇
┌────────────────────────────────────────┐
│                                        │
└────────────────────────────────────────┘
                    ⬇
┌────────────────────────────────────────┐
│                                        │
└────────────────────────────────────────┘
```

Name _____ Date _____

Compare and Contrast Text Pattern

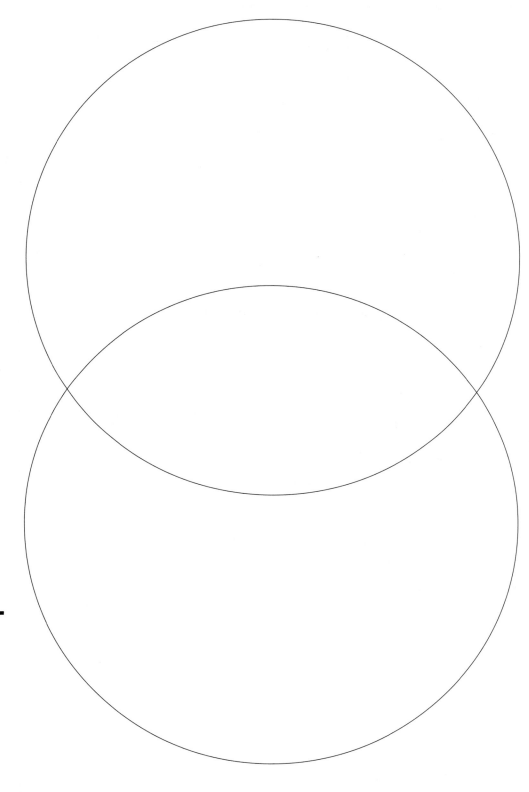

Name _____ Date _____

Comparison and Contrast
Text Pattern

Title

Who or what is being compared?

How are they alike?

How are they different?

From Jerry L. Johns and Roberta L. Berglund, *Strategies for Content Area Learning* (2nd ed.). Copyright © 2006 by Kendall/Hunt Publishing Company (1-800-247-3458, ext. 4). May be reproduced for noncommercial educational purposes. www.kendallhunt.com/readingresources.html

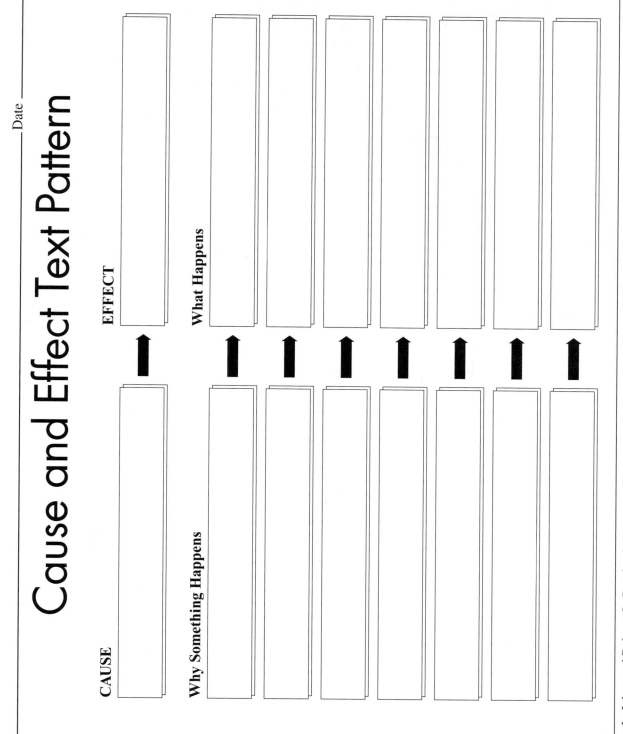

Name _____   Date _____

Cause and Effect Text Pattern

CAUSE

Why Something Happens

EFFECT

What Happens

Name _____ Date _____

Cause and Effect Text Pattern: Chain of Related Events

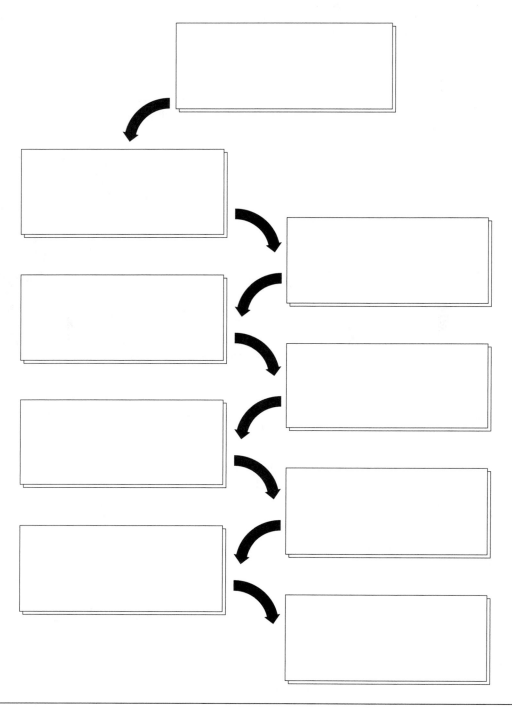

Problem and Solution Text Pattern

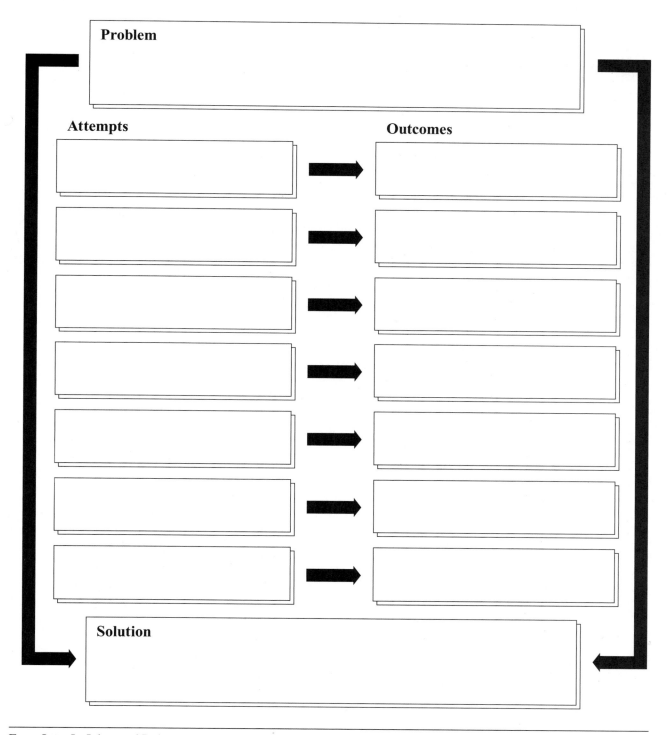